TOLERATING TYRANNY

Security Sought, Freedom Lost

Mike Smith

MSM Publishing
2014

Copyright © 2014 by Mike Smith

All rights reserved. No parts of this book may be reproduced in any form without written permission from the copyright owner.

This book was printed in the United States of America.

Unless otherwise noted, Scripture quotations are from the New American Standard Version of the Bible.

ISBN 978-0-578-14630-0

Additional copies can be purchased at:
www.toleratingtyranny.com

Country Bible Church website:
www.countrybiblechurch.us

Artwork on the cover by Karen Pennison.

Blessed is the nation whose God is the LORD, **Psalm 33:12**

Righteousness exalts a nation, but sin is a disgrace to any people. **Proverbs 14:34**

The words of the wise heard in quietness are better than the shouting of a ruler among fools. **Ecclesiastes 9:17**

CONTENTS

ACKNOWLEDGEMENTS	11
PREFACE	12
CHAPTERS	
1: FACING REALITY	14
Who is the True Patriot?	15
Political Correctness	20
Learn From the Bible	21
Learn From Our Predecessors	23
2: HISTORY TEACHES US TO GUARD AGAINST TYRANNY BACK THEN VS TODAY	25
Dr. David Ramsay's Oration, 1794	26
Regulations	43
3: WHY BIGGER GOVERNMENT?	45
1) Security	49
2) Money	51
3) Ignorance	52
4) Manipulation	54
5) Laziness	56
6) Dependence	57
7) Fear	59
8) Indifference	61
THE MAIN QUESTION:	67

What are Christians to do about government that ignores the Constitution, tramples on their rights, and invades their privacy?

THREE VIEWPOINTS

4: VIEWPOINT 1: Unlimited Authority	68
Is Unlimited Authority Even Reasonable?	69
Does God Require Submission To Tyrants?	74
Should We Trust Our Government?	77
Should We Trust Our Judicial System?	82
Constitutional Amendments That Crippled America	84
Guilty Until Proven Innocent	91

5: <u>VIEWPOINT 2</u>: Limited Authority in Matters of Faith   92
    Going Against Conscience
    The Religion-Government Link   95
    Is Government or Conscience Superior?   100
    Duty to Submit Ends Where Tyranny Begins   109
    The Natural Law of God   111

6: <u>VIEWPOINT 3</u>: Limited Authority in Matters of
                      Faith and Freedom   115
    Declaration of Independence Citations   117
    Our Rights Come From God   118
    Government is to Protect and Secure Our Rights   119
    The Right to Alter or Abolish Government   121

7: ROMANS 13   123
    Misunderstood & Misapplied   124
    <u>Romans 13:1</u> Submission to God's Delegated Authorities   127
    <u>Romans 13:2</u> Punishment for Resisting Legitimate Authority   137
    <u>Romans 13:3</u> Good Rulers Respect Good Behavior   140
                     What is Good Behavior?   142
                     What is Bad Behavior?   145
    <u>Romans 13:4</u> Ministers of God for Good   146
    <u>Romans 13:5</u> Submit for Conscience Sake   156
                     Obeying Conscience   157
                     The Nuremburg Trials   159
                     An Evil King Not Resisted   162
    <u>Romans 13:6</u> Paying Taxes   163
                     Support for Devoted Servants of God   167
    <u>Romans 13:7</u> Render Unto Caesar... Who is Caesar?   168

8: OBJECTIONS TO RESISTING TYRANNY   172
    1) Christians Should Avoid Worldly Entanglements
    2) We Should Follow First Century Christians' Example   175
    3) Pastors Should Stay Out of Politics   176
        Pastors, Politics, and the Black-Robed Regiment   177
    4) Government Should Be Involved in Child-Rearing   182
    5) Loyalty to Country Requires Submission to Government   184

9: <u>OPTIONS FOR KEEPING FREEDOM</u>	187
Meekness If Possible	
Refuse to Turn the Other Cheek	188
Voting the Scoundrels Out of Office	191
Constitutional Grand Juries &Trial Juries	195
Interposition Is Preferable	199
Nullification or Secession	202
10. <u>RESISTANCE IF NECESSARY</u>	204
Did Jesus Resist?	
Examples of Biblical Civil Disobedience	209
Resisting Tyranny Is Not Revolution	213
The 2nd Amendment	217
Genocide Statistics Over the Past Century	220
Gun Control	221
A Brave, Constitutional Sheriff in Florida	223
Jesus' Unjust Arrest	226
Men of Renown Resisted Tyranny	231
11: <u>CONCLUSION</u>	238
EPILOGUE	244
BIBLIOGRAPHY	246

ACKNOWLEDGMENTS

I would like to thank my Lord and Savior, Jesus Christ, for giving me the knowledge, motivation and opportunity to write this book. I thank my two great mentors, my father, Charles K. Smith Jr., and Robert B. Thieme Jr. who was the pastor of Berachah Church in Houston, Texas for over fifty years.

I would also like to thank those who took time out of their busy schedules to edit this book. I certainly appreciate the editing, patience and dedication of my lovely and devoted wife, Kari. Then I wish to extend my gratitude to other editing done by Kim Llewellyn, Candace Thieme-Schulz, and Margaret Kathman.

My deep appreciation is extended to Dr. Jim Brettell and Pastor John Eichmann for their wise suggestions and encouragement.

And I would also like to thank all those at Country Bible Church for their support, their eagerness to learn the Word of God, and their love.

PREFACE

Everyone I know is very disturbed about what is happening to our country. They see their freedoms, privacy, and property slipping away and they don't know what to do about it. They're looking for answers because they have lost faith in our government. They have become exasperated with the same old pseudo-solutions and platitudes offered by politicians and the media.

Many seek the opinions of family, friends, and political pundits but wind up confused, still not being sure what they should do. Some aren't even open to discussing the issue. And while most have very strong feelings about *what* they believe, they have never stopped to ask themselves *why* they believe it.

The key to finding the right answers is to first ask the right questions, like this one for example: "Are we required to submit unconditionally to every government demand, even if it is unconstitutional or immoral?"

Many Christians believe the Bible would have us answer "yes" to this question, but are they right? Does the Bible require unconditional submission to government? *Tolerating Tyranny* addresses this issue head-on and explains the proper relationship between people and their government from both a biblical and historical perspective.

This book asks questions that we all should be asking and offers hope from a viewpoint that many haven't considered. It conveys an important message that Americans desperately need to hear. It is relevant, thought-provoking, challenging, and a sure-fire confidence-builder. It provides answers for freedom-loving people who are seeking truth.

It is important that we remain objective and open-minded as we delve into the Bible and history to determine how to get our country back. God is pleased when we set aside all bias and presuppositions so that we can simply, calmly and rationally discuss these crucial matters.

"Come now, and let us reason together", says the Lord... **Isaiah 1:18**

CHAPTER 1

FACING REALITY

There is no honor in tolerating tyranny; it is neither virtuous nor patriotic. Abuse of authority is dreadful wherever it is found, but it is especially distressing when it occurs in our own government.

People are afraid to talk about politics, government, or religion because they consider it to be impolite to even bring up such issues as it might offend someone. It's true that few topics are more controversial than these, but ask yourself: Is it really wise to avoid discussing matters as important as the Bible and our government at this particular time in our history?

As long as we limit our conversations to superficial trivialities, adopt a politically correct vocabulary, and ignore the imminent danger of being enslaved by our government, true freedom will remain beyond our grasp.

The more oppressive our government becomes, the more we, who love freedom, feel compelled to act. But what can we do? What should we do? Everyone wants to do what is right, and Christians want to do what is biblically correct, but before we turn to our Bibles and history books to find out what that is, let's start by asking ourselves some disturbing questions we are inclined to avoid, such as:

What should we do now that our government is ignoring the Constitution, invading our privacy, perverting justice in the courts, demanding exorbitant taxes, promoting immorality and constructing a police state? Must we obey every corrupt and abusive government dictate without question? Does the Bible require this of Christians?

WHO IS THE TRUE PATRIOT?

Some people are very uncomfortable with these kinds of questions and would rather pretend things aren't really all that bad. They feel it is their patriotic duty to staunchly defend their government under any and all circumstances no matter how corrupt or despotic it has become. They comfort themselves with patriotic slogans like, "America, the land of the free and the home of the brave", while deep down, they know it's no longer true. We are becoming "the land of the fee and the home of the slave.

Victims who suffer at the hands of an abusive authority are usually frightened and often have a deep sense of shame about their situation. Many wives find it hard to admit that they are married to a criminally-abusive husband; children often hide the abuse they suffer from others; and citizens continue to be loyal and submissive to a government that oppresses and enslaves them. Surely the normal rules of submission that God set in place do not apply in such situations.

One of the strongest detriments to liberty is the subjective attitude of denial. Some people will never acknowledge just how far the government has intruded into their lives or how many calculated steps it has taken to maintain its control over them.

However, to even suggest that America is losing her greatness would send some people into a rage. These people are in denial and probably don't realize it, but if they did, chances are they would never admit it.

They would feel guilty or disloyal for even thinking that the nation they have long revered, routinely violates their rights to the point that it is no longer worthy of allegiance. Such feelings of guilt and disloyalty are misplaced because there is a big difference between loyalty to country and loyalty to an oppressive government.

One does not have to love his government in order to love his country. Millions of Americans love their country but have come to deplore their government. When a government becomes a self-perpetuating "corporation" that serves itself and denies individual rights, it no longer deserves allegiance or loyalty.

Those who don't understand this principle believe it is wrong to criticize Congress or the President no matter how many unconstitutional laws and unprecedented regulations and edicts they impose on us. In their misguided zeal, they castigate and brand as "traitor" anyone who dares to say America has lost its way and is becoming a police state.

They don't realize that they are giving total allegiance to the state when it rightfully belongs to God alone. It is this kind of absolute, unquestioning allegiance to government that enables the unscrupulous scoundrels in office to increase their power and control over those they have pledged to serve.

"...it is possible for love of country to take the place of love for God. The flag should symbolize God's love for America; but it is possible to get so wrapped up in the flag that we can no longer see God. When that happens, we have rejected the Christian view of patriotism and have embraced the pagan view of the state: that the State is God! Misguided patriotism can also blind us to our country's short-comings. It can stifle criticism and cause us to regard dissent as unpatriotic. But that's not true patriotism." [1]

Is the true patriot one who defends the oppressive acts of his government or one who speaks out against them? Who is the traitor? Is it the citizen who refuses to submit to unconstitutional laws, or is it the politician who passes those unconstitutional laws?

"The idea that we must be patriotic of [to] the State itself, rather than the freedom we hold dear, is a lie." [2]

In 1904, Mark Twain said, "In the beginning of a change, the PATRIOT is a scarce man, and brave and hated and scorned. When his cause succeeds, the timid join him, for then it cost nothing to be a PATRIOT."

Repeating a patriotic slogan or chanting, "USA!" "USA!" at an international sporting event may temporarily suppress anxiety concerning government overreach but it will not relieve the gnawing reality that our country is no longer worthy of praise. One can ignore the facts, but not their consequences.

The America that once was, is now gone, and to pretend that our nation is still strong and great will only

---

[1] John Eidsmoe, *God and Caesar, Biblical Faith and Political Action,* Wipf and Stock Publishers, p. 41.

[2] Gavin Siem, "Detained Because of the Constitution?" Mike Maharrey, *Activism, Federal Power,* 6-4-12.

hasten its demise. We cannot restore our nation if we continue to pretend that all is well.

It is very enlightening to listen to men like Mark Levin who aren't afraid to describe our nation as it truly is. His description of our federal government's abuses can be found in his latest book, *The Liberty Amendments*:

> "What was to be a relatively innocuous federal government operating from a defined enumeration of specific grants of power, has become an ever-present and unaccountable force. It is the nation's largest creditor, debtor, lender, employer, consumer, contractor, grantor, property owner, tenant, insurer, health-care provider, and pension guarantor. Moreover, with its aggrandized police powers, what it does not control directly it bans or mandates by regulation.
>
> For example, the federal government regulates most things in your bathroom, laundry room, and kitchen as well as the mortgage on your house. It designs your automobile and dictates the kind of fuel it uses. It regulates your baby's toys, crib, and stroller; plans your children's school curriculum and lunch menu; and administers their student loans in college. At your place of employment, the federal government oversees everything from the racial, gender, and age diversity of the workforce to the hours, wages, and benefits paid. Indeed the question is not what the federal government regulates, but what does it not." [3]

This describes a government that has lost sight of its purpose which is to protect the freedoms and rights of

---

[3] Mark Levin, *The Liberty Amendments*, Threshold Editions, 2013, pp. 6-7.

the people while administering justice to those who violate them. The first ten "amendments" to the Constitution known as "The Bill of Rights" are actually constraints placed on our federal government so it will not intrude into our private affairs or infringe on our God-given, individual rights.

However, the Bill of Rights and the Constitution are now blatantly ignored by the very ones who took a solemn oath, "...so help me God", to uphold and defend them. The result has been disastrous. The people who were once masters over the government they created now find themselves the servants of that government.

> "Our once carefully limited and restrictive civil government now claims the unbiblical right of 'playing God' by invading our homes, our schools, our churches, and our business, financial, and personal lives. *It has become a secular god to whom all must bow.* No sphere, not even one small niche, is sacred any more from the strong hand of civil government as the humanistic state attempts to care for people from the cradle to the grave." [4]

It's hard to face the truth that our country is no longer what it once was. Americans used to be self-reliant, industrious, inventive and charitable, and didn't depend on government to fix their problems. We once followed a standard of morality and privacy accepted by the majority. Rules, regulations, codes, statutes and laws didn't stifle our freedom nor were people intimidated

---

[4] Tom Rose, *Our Reconstruction and the American Republic, Christianity and Civilization,* Geneva Divinity School Press, 1983, p.309 (emphasis in original).

by government bullies. We were not forced to accept a new world order whose goal is to dissolve our national sovereignty along with our individual freedoms.

POLITICAL CORRECTNESS

But now our words must be chosen carefully to make sure they line up with whatever the media and our government consider acceptable. America has become a politically correct nation where saying something that offends someone is a cardinal sin. And if a criminal is politically incorrect while committing a crime, he can be convicted of a "hate crime" and receive a much harsher sentence simply because the crime was motivated by hate. Hate is a mental attitude sin and is no more of a crime than lust, anger, or covetousness, but in politically correct America, people are being punished for what they think. How long will it be before people are arrested for being jealous, selfish, or ungrateful?

> "There are a lot of reasons why the U.S. is becoming less appealing with each passing day. In addition to our economic problems, crime is on the rise in our cities, our liberties and freedoms are being eroded at a frightening pace, political correctness is wildly out of control, and our corrupt politicians continue to make things even worse." [5]

Many Christians live in fear of expressing their faith because if someone is offended, there could be severe repercussions. Fines and punishments could be right around the corner for anyone who expresses the biblical

---

[5] *The Economic Collapse Blog,* March 7, 2013.

view on issues such as homosexuality. Pastors in other countries are already being charged with hate crimes for calling homosexuality a sin.

Christmas trees, the Ten Commandments, and prayer have been banned in courthouses and schools, Bibles, Christian music, and jewelry with crosses are also banned from many workplaces and schools, and wearing clothing with religious words or images on them have also been prohibited in several places.

How did the once-proud symbols of Christianity become so offensive? There are a multitude of reasons and they all are inextricably linked to the fact that man's laws have become more and more at odds with God's laws.

LEARN FROM THE BIBLE

Where do we go to find out how to get the government's enormous nose out of our business? Who should we consult? Wouldn't it be a good idea to go to the supreme authority of the universe to find out what He has to say? Absolutely! The Bible can be trusted because it is inspired by God and is the ultimate source of truth:

> *All scripture is given by inspiration of God, and is profitable for doctrine, for reproof, for correction, for instruction in righteousness....* **2 Tim. 3:16**.

The Bible is the primary resource used in the pages that follow to address the challenges before us. After all, it provides everything we need because it is the operating manual for the human race.

...seeing that His divine power has granted to us everything pertaining to life and godliness through the true knowledge of Him [acquired from the Bible].... **_2 Peter 1:3_**

"You will want a book that contains not man's thoughts, but God's, not a book that may amuse you, but a book that can save you...." [6]

And from it we learn that everyone and everything is subject to God's impeccable sovereign authority. He ordained government to be an integral part of His wonderful plan for this world. So, you can rest-assured that this book is neither anti-government nor is it anti-authority. On the contrary, it is very pro good government and pro fair authority.

The structure of authority that God established for mankind is the bond that holds marriages, families, and societies together. Just as gravity brings order and stability to the universe, authority brings order and stability to our lives. Without it, there would be utter chaos.

Since God has delegated authority to imperfect humans, it is inevitable that they will be less than perfect in their application of it and will abuse their authority sooner or later. God expects us to tolerate certain foibles and short-comings in those who have authority over us, but He never commands us to tolerate abuse.

There is a point where forbearance and toleration are no longer a virtue, when authority is no longer legitimate, and when submission is no longer required.

---

[6] John Selden, *Dictionary of Burning Words of Brilliant Writers: A Cyclopedia from the Literature of All Ages* (1895), p. 29.

Government can become so corrupted by evil that continued allegiance and submission to it becomes evil as well.

If we are to turn this nation around, pastors must teach this biblical truth to their congregations and we must communicate it to our family and friends.

> *And these words which I command you today shall be in your heart. 7) You shall teach them diligently to your children, and shall talk of them when you sit in your house, when you walk by the way, when you lie down, and when you rise up.* **Deuteronomy 6:6-7**

Moses commanded the Israelites to not only meditate on the biblical precepts the Lord gave them, but to diligently teach them to their children so that each generation would be right with God and enjoy national security and prosperity There was a time when this type of instruction routinely took place in our churches and schools, but it is hard to find today. The fundamental knowledge that is essential for maintaining individual rights and freedoms comes from the Bible and from history, but this knowledge is no longer being passed down to younger generations.

> "Go, call thy sons, instruct them what a debt they owe to their ancestors, and make them swear to pay it, by transmitting down entire those sacred rights to which themselves were born." [7]

LEARN FROM OUR PREDECESSORS

We can also learn from those who have come before us. Therefore, quotes taken from historians, political figures, historical documents, the founding fathers, authors,

---

[7] Patrick Henry, Quoted by Norine Dixon Campbell, *Patrick Henry: Patriot and Statesman* (Delvin Adair Co. 1969) p. 222.

pastors, and theologians are included as well.

We learn from them that we had better stop shirking our responsibility and start holding our leaders accountable. If we know what's good for us, we will turn to our Bibles and history books to learn what we must do to get our country back on track. The potential for America to return to greatness remains, but it will not happen until we remove the paralyzing chokehold the government has on us.

And for that to happen, ignorance and apathy must be vanquished, and we must start trusting in the promises of God rather than Washington D.C. to save us. It will take courage, knowledge, determination, and prayer to change the disastrous direction in which we are headed.

If our government is returned to its constitutional limits, and its servants develop a new respect for the Bill of Rights and abide by it, then it will function once again as a minister of God for good. Only then will we enjoy the blessings of freedom for which our founders gave their lives.

CHAPTER 2

HISTORY TEACHES US TO GUARD AGAINST TYRANNY

BACK THEN VS TODAY

God led the Israelites out of Egypt and they became a theocracy which means that God Himself was their King. He gave them the Mosaic Law to help maintain order and freedom, but they became discontent and wanted to be like other nations who were ruled by kings. God warned them that a human king would eventually abuse them, but they wouldn't listen and continued to insist on having a fallible man rather than an infallible God rule over them. So Saul became the first king over Israel, 1 Sam. 8:5-22, and of course, it wasn't long before the people realized the truth in God's warning.

Throughout the ages, people have struggled with kings, prime ministers, potentates, Caesars, czars, dictators, and presidents who ruled over them. A few were benevolent and some were fair, but most of them could not control their lust for wealth and power. They used their position of authority for their own purpose and benefit and eventually became overbearing tyrants.

People lived for centuries under what came to be known as "the divine right of kings". This practice asserted the belief that God gave kings unlimited authority and required the people to submit unconditionally to their will. The well-being of the people depended on the character and temperament of their ruler.

We can look back at the colonists and see that they wanted to separate from England because they recognized that rights come from God and not from kings, parliaments, or governments. Furthermore, they understood that these rights are unalienable, meaning that they are inviolable and cannot be transferred or abridged without the consent of the individual. So with great courage and confidence that their cause was righteous, they declared their independence and freedom from the oppressive British king.

At that time, Great Britain was the most powerful nation in the world, so the king and parliament were aghast at these upstarts who dared to defy the authority of their king. A bloody war ensued and no one thought the colonies had even a remote chance of victory. The "Revolutionary War" lasted over seven years, but finally, the British troops left New York Harbor on November 23, 1783, at long last leaving the thirteen colonies free and independent.

DR. DAVID RAMSAY'S ORATION, 1794

On July 4, 1794, eighteen years after the Declaration of Independence was signed, the leader of the Senate, Dr. David Ramsay, gave the first Independence Day oration describing the state of the union. He had been a field surgeon during the war and was a noted historian after the war. Dr. Ramsay detailed the principles of our government that were constructed to counter the tyrannical effects of the monarchic governments of Europe:

> "In the United States, the blessings of society are enjoyed with the least possible relinquishment of personal liberty. We have hit the happy medium between despotism and anarchy. Every citizen is perfectly free of the will of every other citizen while all are equally subject to the laws. Among us, no one can exercise any authority by virtue of birth. All start equal in the race of life. No man is born a legislator. *We are not bound by any laws but those to which we have consented....*" [8]

TODAY: We are loaded down every year with thousands of codes, rules, and regulations that carry the force of law. We have no say in the making of them, don't even know what most of them are, and yet we are expected to submit to all of them whether we consent to them or not. Why? What compels us as sovereign, free people to consent to any code, rule, or regulation that goes against the Constitution, the Bible, or our conscience? We need to raise our voices in protest over anything that violates our freedom, otherwise, the government will keep on taking our silence as consent. And history teaches us that consent breeds corruption over time.

BACK THEN: Ramsay continued by describing the frugality and conscientiousness of governing officials.

> "We are not called upon to pay our money to support the idleness and extravagance of court favorites. No burdens are imposed on us but such as the public good requires." [9]

---

[8] David Barton, *"An Oration by Dr. David Ramsay 1794',* Celebrate Liberty! Famous Patriotic Speeches and Sermons*, WallBuilder Press, 2003, pp. 19-29 [emphasis added].

[9] *ibid*

TODAY: Have politicians become extravagant court favorites?

They go on trips or "junkets" at the public's expense, and they pass "boondoggles" which are bills that fund wasteful and impractical projects to gain favor with the voters. They have given themselves extremely lavish retirements that are referred to as "golden parachutes". Former congressman, Ron Paul, was at least one who refused to participate in the congressional pension system, labeling it as immoral.

BACK THEN: Ramsay continued,

> "The liberty of the press is enjoyed in these States in a manner that is unknown in other countries. Each citizen thinks what he pleases and speaks and writes what he thinks." [10]

TODAY: The freedom of speech that was once enjoyed by the press and by citizens is quickly disappearing. The press often hits a stone wall when trying to get the truth from government sources while Christians are censored and even prevented from expressing their faith at graduation ceremonies and sporting events.

Some local governments like the one in San Antonio, Texas have passed laws that punish city employees who refuse to accept homosexuality, alleging that they are guilty of discrimination. The same is true for businesses working with the city. This is a blatant assault on the 1st Amendment's free exercise of religion clause. They are arrogantly and erroneously punishing the free exercise of thought, speech, writing and religion by calling it discrimination. Shame on them!

BACK THEN: Ramsay wrote:

---

[10] *ibid*

"So great is the responsibility of men in high stations among us that it is the fashion to rule well. We read of the rapacity [corruption], cruelty, and oppression of men in power but our rulers seem for the most part to be exempt from these vices." [11]

TODAY: Corruption is rampant in our government. Scandals abound involving high-ranking officials in all areas of government:

- The *"Fast and Furious" Scandal* where our government sold thousands of guns to drug cartels in Mexico.

- The *Benghazi Scandal* where four Americans died in a terrorist raid on our embassy in Libya because political expediency and cover-up was more important than demanding justice for American lives.

- The *Obamacare Rollout Computer Scandal* where hundreds of millions were wasted on a flawed computer system that left millions of Americans in the lurch with no health care insurance.

- The *IRS Targeting the Tea Party Scandal* and subsequent *Investigation Cover-Up Scandal* involving the loss of thousands of potentially incriminating IRS e-mails.

- The *NSA's Massive Data-Mining Scandal* where the privacy of Americans is invaded on a massive scale.

- The *Nevada-Bundy-BLM Scandal* where armed BLM agents threatened, bullied, and tasered unarmed US citizens.

- The *Prisoner Swap Scandal* recently where five top, high-ranking terrorists were released from prison

---

[11] *ibid*

to secure the release of one American soldier who has been accused of desertion.

- The **VA scandal** where many veterans died waiting for medical care while V.A. bureaucrats received big bonuses.
- The **Texas Border Scandal** where estimates of 35 thousand foreign children and adults are pouring into the US illegally every month, and many of them have criminal records and diseases. Our government is assisting them in their criminal activity by sending them to various cities across the country at tax-payers expense. This is an unmitigated disaster.

These are just a few of the current scandals that have actually been uncovered which our president has dismissed as "phony scandals". People are no longer shocked by malfeasance in government. They have come to accept the outrages committed by governing officials as "normal".

BACK THEN: Ramsay related his perception of their leaders.

"Such are the effects of governments formed on equal principles that men in authority cannot easily forget that they are the servants of the community over which they preside. Our rulers, taken from the people (and at stated periods returning to them) have the strongest incitement to make the public will their guide and the public good their end." [12]

The founding fathers were skilled in differing occupations such as farmers, merchants, financiers, scientists, doctors, and other jobs that they returned to after their congressional sessions ended. They were in touch with the people they represented and did not sequester themselves in granite Capitol buildings.

---
[12] *ibid*

TODAY: Career politicians have become the norm. An example is former Sen. Robert Byrd from West Virginia who was a U.S. Representative for 6 years and a U.S. Senator for 51 years. One can acquire tremendous power and influence over such a long period of time and easily forget that he is just a servant and not the master of the people.

BACK THEN: Ramsay said,
"It is one of the peculiar privileges we enjoy in consequence of independence that no individual, no party interest, no foreign influence, can plunge us into war... Think of the cruel war now carrying on by kings and nobles against the equal rights of man, call to mind the slaughtered thousands whose blood is daily shedding on the plains of Europe, and let your daily tribute of thanks ascend to the Common Parent of the Universe [God] Who has established you in a separate government exempt from participating in these horrid scenes..." [13]

Had the colonists remained in Europe, they would have been conscripted to fight in wars just because their king had a dispute with another king. But since America's new government was established on a written constitution rather than on the fickle notions of a king, her men were exempt from fighting frivolous and horrendous wars. Instead, they kept their noses in their own business and their focus on protecting their own country from foreign attack.

The founders knew well the horrible suffering and financial ruin that occurs when one man has the power to thrust a nation into war. That is why Article 1, Section 8 was included in the Constitution which requires a declaration of war from Congress before going to war.

---

[13] *ibid*

TODAY: Congress has made no declaration of war since WW II. All of the unimaginable suffering, loss of life and tremendous financial cost in the Korean, Viet Nam, Iraq, and Afghanistan Wars may have been averted or mitigated if Congress would have adhered to our Constitution.

> "There was a day when U.S. troops were expected to fight and die for liberty. Now it's for interests ... In his 1993 inaugural speech President Clinton declared boldly, 'When our vital interests are challenged, or the will of the international community is defied, we will act, with peaceful diplomacy whenever possible, with force when necessary." [14]

BACK THEN: Ramsay recorded the unbelievable statistics about the freedoms they enjoyed because they did not have to finance an out-of-control government.

> "Upon an average, five of our citizens do not pay as much to the support of government as one European subject. The whole sum expended in administering the public affairs of the United States is not equal to the fourth part of what is annually spent in supporting one crowned head in Europe...

> "In these States, property and personal rights are well secured. Time would fail to enumerate all the superior advantages our citizens enjoy under that free government to which independence gave birth...

> "Sovereignty rests in ourselves; and instead of receiving the privileges of free citizens as a boon [favor] from the hands of our rulers, we defined their powers by a constitution of our own framing which prescribed to

---

[14] Richard J. Maybury, *Ancient Rome, How It Affects You Today,* Bluestocking Press, 2004, p. 52.

them that thus far they might go but no farther. All power not thus expressly delegated [to the federal government] is retained [by the sovereign States and the people themselves]." [15]

Ramsay was referring to the 10th Amendment to the Constitution that keeps the federal government from overstepping its authority and forcing its will on the States and the people.

TODAY: Several States today believe the federal government has overstepped its constitutional authority by forcing Obamacare on us and are now passing laws to prohibit its implementation. People are appalled that our president has given Congress and its staff sizable reductions in what they themselves will have to pay for the deplorable "Affordable Care Act" (ACA) that they enacted. So they will not have to suffer under that dreadful freedom-destroying law they forced on the rest of us.

"...That document [the Constitution] nowhere grants any powers even remotely resembling those claimed for ObamaCare, the ACA represents an egregious violation of the Rule of Law and an enormous usurpation of power. A federal law commanding Americans to buy a government-mandated product and outlawing our current means of providing for our own health is so transparently unconstitutional and hostile to our liberty that it is incomprehensible that we would allow it to stand." [16]

BACK THEN: People were very grateful to God for the

---

[15] David Barton, "An Oration by Dr. David Ramsay 1794", *Celebrate Liberty! Famous Patriotic Speeches and Sermons.*

[16] William Jasper, "ObamaCare's Unfixable Fatal Flaws", *The New American*, Dec. 2, 2013, p. 44.

blessings of freedom and security they enjoyed from having a well-ordered and efficient government.

> "We ought, in the first place, to be grateful to the all-wise Disposer of Events Who has given us so great a portion of political happiness. To possess such a country with the blessings of liberty and peace together with that security of person and property which results from a well-ordered, efficient government is, or ought to be, [a] matter of constant thankfulness." [17]

TODAY: Political happiness? Our political system is so divided by partisan politicians and so corrupted by the lust for money that people no longer trust it and doubt whether it can, or should, survive.

Blessings of liberty? Ha! We are cursed with massive government regulations, OSHA, EPA, IRS, police checkpoints on highways, government mandated insurance, indefinite detainment of citizens, water boarding, and hate crime laws.

Security of person and property? No one escapes the TSA groping at airports, full body scans, warrantless searches, or massive data-mining by NSA. Gun control laws put the people's lives at risk and property taxes put their property in jeopardy.

Well-ordered and efficient government? Who in their right mind would say this about ours today? How many of you remember LBJ's "Great Society"? Eliminating poverty and stopping racial injustice were two of his main reform goals that were forced on us. Hundreds of billions were spent on high-rise government housing projects for the poor, and children were bused against their will to schools chosen by the State in order to

---
[17] *ibid*

achieve an arbitrary racial balance. Both were colossal failures. Efficient, well-ordered governments do not engage in such foolhardy, unconstitutional endeavors nor do they carry an outrageous $17 trillion dollar national debt.

BACK THEN: Ramsay continued to impart wisdom as he described what our country was like.

> "Ignorance is the enemy of liberty, the nurse of despotism… Had I a voice that could be heard from New Hampshire to Georgia, it should be exerted in urging the necessity of disseminating virtue and knowledge among our citizens. On this subject, the policy of the eastern States is well worthy of imitation. The wise people of that extremity of the Union never form a new township without making arrangements that secure to its inhabitants the instruction of youth and the public preaching of the Gospel. Hence their children are early taught to know their rights and to respect themselves." [18]

TODAY: There aren't many parents, pastors, or school teachers teaching young people about their God-given rights, principles of freedom, or how to be responsible, self-reliant adults. Young people are no longer taught that all political power is inherent in the people, and any government that becomes destructive of their rights forfeits its authority.

BACK THEN: Ramsay's speech continued,

> "Animated with this noble ambition, the superior happiness of our country will amply repay us for the blood and treasure which independence has cost. May that ambition fire our breast, and may that

---
[18] *ibid*

happiness increase and know no end, till time shall be no more." [19]

TODAY: Much has changed but not for the better.

Think of all the people who have given their lives or given up their loved ones to secure our freedoms from the founding of our country until now and all of the sacrifices that have been made by so many for the cause of liberty. Now we're seeing it all being squandered away by a relatively few, exceedingly evil people for their own personal gain. This should create within us an anger, a righteous indignation that is strong enough to destroy any apathy or indifference in our hearts. It should motivate us to demand that our representatives in government respect their oaths to the Constitution or remove them from office.

Many Americans depend on the government to take care of them. They expect, and sometimes demand that the government provide them with food stamps, child care, education, housing, funds to rebuild after natural disasters, etc. They have forgotten what it means to be self-reliant and independent; perhaps they never experienced what that is like, or maybe they are just plain ole' lazy.

Changes have come incrementally over the years as people have let their guard down and become more and more complacent.

BACK THEN: A mere hundred years ago, people had money with intrinsic value such as gold and silver coins and there were:

    No property taxes
    No inheritance taxes
    No capital gains taxes

---

[19] *ibid*

No local or city taxes
No county taxes
No social security taxes
No school taxes,
No state income taxes,
No federal income taxes,
No Medicare taxes,
No state and local sales taxes,
No luxury taxes,
No estate sales taxes,
No unemployment taxes,
No telephone taxes,
No gasoline taxes,
No permit fees,
No registration fees
No inspection fees…

TODAY: Our older population has seen a multitude of unwanted changes occur over the years, and the huge transfer of their wealth to the government has had devastating results.

"With the passing of almost unlimited taxing and money-creating power into the hands of people at the central government, the American people have been subsequently conditioned financially to look to the national government as the Great Provider. They now turn to Washington for the meeting of all their material needs and to solve all their problems. In short, the American people have eschewed Jesus' instructions to pray to our heavenly Father for our daily bread (Matt. 6:11), and they have allowed the national government to become their god. In fleeing self-responsibility, they have set up the national State as their secular god. As a people, Americans have become idolatrous! …The burning question which faces concerned Americans, especially [Christian] Americans, is this: What can be done about the disturbing unbiblical growth of absolutist and tyrannical civil government in America? What can be done to reclaim the original American Christian dream of individual freedom and self-responsibility before God, which is the underlying principle upon which our American Republic was founded?" [20]

BACK THEN: It was the pastors of Colonial America who taught not only the biblical perspective of the gift of salvation through the atoning work of Jesus Christ, but also the practical application of biblical principles for every area of life including the institution of civil government. The Reverend Samuel West in "An Election Sermon" preaching to the Council and House of Representatives of the Massachusetts Bay Colony, May 29, 1776, said:

> "Our obligation to promote the public good extends as much to the opposing every exertion of arbitrary power that is injurious to the state as it does to the submitting to good and wholesome laws. *No man, therefore, can be a good member of the community that is not as zealous to oppose tyranny as he is ready to obey magistracy."* [Emphasis added]

The pastors led the way in preparing people to deal with tyranny in colonial days as they should be doing today.

TODAY: Most pastors do not teach the whole realm of doctrine contained in the Scriptures, nor do they address

---

[20] Tom Rose, "On Reconstruction and the American Republic", *Christianity and Civilization, The Journal of Christian Reconstruction,* Vol. 5, No. 1 (Summer © 1978).

government overreach because they either don't know the biblical principles concerning it or they're afraid of being scolded by their congregations for being too political.

"America needs in the worst way stalwart preachers and expounders of the faith who will carefully and systematically instruct the people in the biblical principles of civil government and who will fearlessly oppose as anti-biblical the current growth of despotic and tyrannical civil government at any level, but especially at the national level, where it is now concentrating into a Babel-like power." [21]

BACK THEN: Just compare the past 70-100 years to the present and consider some of the changes that have taken place:

- We called men "<u>Peace</u> Officers", who protected people and kept the peace. We respected them and appreciated their concern for us as we do now. However, it appears that the focus has changed from keeping the peace to enforcing the law. So "<u>Peace</u> Officers" have turned into "<u>Police</u> Officers" tasked with enforcing revenue-generating, arbitrary statutes.

- **TODAY**: There is an exceedingly dangerous precedent being set when local police forces and state police agencies around the country unite with federal military forces, not only to maintain order in natural disasters, but also in domestic disruptions. And unlike police officers whose job is to protect citizens

---

[21] Tom Rose, *"On Reconstruction and the American Republic"*, *(Christianity & Civilization, vol. 2, The Theology of Christian Resistance, "On Reconstruction and the American Republic")*.

and keep the peace, soldiers are warriors, trained to kill. Putting soldiers who are trained for combat into a civilian-policing situation can result in serious collateral damage to the lives and freedoms of Americans.

Police swat teams and the law enforcement arm of federal agencies look and act more and more like combat troops. They wear helmets, body armor, and carry military style automatic weapons.

- **BACK THEN:** No one celebrated diversity or multi-culturalism. People did not want to be identified as African-American, Irish-American, Polish-American, Asian-American, Egyptian-American, Mexican-American, German-American, Italian-American, English-American, or Jewish-American. Cultural distinctions didn't matter. They just wanted to be known as "Americans".

- Immigrants entered our country lawfully and were eager to learn English. They yearned to assimilate into our culture.

- People enjoyed a greater sense of personal freedom from government. There were no surveillance cameras, no eavesdropping, no wiretaps or searches made without a warrant, and no routine pat-downs or full-body scans.

- There were no welfare programs, food stamps or FEMA. Family, friends, churches and charitable organizations took care of people in need, not the government!

- There was no EPA, OSHA, FBI, CIA, BATF, DHS, NATO, SEATO, UN, USDA, BLM, HUD, CPS, FDA, FCC, FTC, INS, DOT, DOE, DOA, IRS, IMF, and no World Bank or World Court.

"Nowhere does the [U. S.] Constitution authorize federal involvement in education, in health-care, in food safety, in environmental regulations, in stock markets, in the automobile industry, in the insurance sector, in the creation and maintenance of national parks, in the regulation of pharmaceuticals, in the legalization (or illegalization) of drugs, in the investigation or prosecution of crimes other than treason or piracy, in the regulation of firearms and ownership, in the providing of retirement insurance (Social Security), in the stipulation of minimum wages, or in any host of other things deemed 'essential'." [22]

- Parents either home-schooled their children, provided a tutor, sent them to aunts and uncles, or enrolled them in a private school. Some communities had public schools, but there was little or no government intrusion and control until the early 1960s.

- No one needed a license to hunt, fish, drive, or carry a gun.

LICENSE: "A permission granted by competent authority to engage in a business or occupation or in **an activity otherwise unlawful**." [emphasis added] Merriam-Webster.com

Is getting married a crime? Is it unlawful? Of course not. Even the U.S. Supreme Court recognizes that fact:

"Skinner v. Oklahoma ex rel. Williamson, **316 U.S.535 (1942).** Marriage is 'one of the basic civil rights of man' and 'fundamental to the very existence and survival of the race'."

---

[22] Charles Scaliger, "Lessons From the Shutdown", *The New American*, Nov. 18, 2013, p. 21.

"Loving v. Virginia, **388 U.S.1 (1967).** The freedom to marry has long been recognized as one of the vital personal rights essential to the orderly pursuit of happiness by free men."

Since getting married is not a crime or unlawful, why do couples feel compelled to purchase a license from the government when they get married? There was no such thing as a marriage license in the United States until April of 1856 and issuing them did not become a common practice till much later. Prior to then, people recorded their marriages in their Bibles and the State stayed out of it.

"The marriage license is a Secular Contract between the parties and the State. The State is the principal party in that Secular Contract. The husband and wife are secondary or inferior parties." [23]

TODAY: Just about everything and everybody must be licensed:

Auctioneers	Barbers	Beauticians	Animal Groomers
Boats	Brokers	Fish Buyers	Bail Bondsmen
Boxers	Kick Boxers	Midwives	Exterminators
Manicurists	Marriages	Masseuses	Food Inspectors
Motels	Plumbers	Pool Cleaning	Motor Vehicles
Morticians	Motorcycles	Pump Installers	Snowmobiles
Animal Massagers			

That's right. The Department of Health in the State of Washington requires a license for massaging animals.

---

[23] "How Did Gov't. Get Involved in Marriage?" www.alimonyreform.org/content/articles/How%20Did%20Government%20

This is just a short portion of a list that has over four hundred occupations or possessions requiring a license.

Many well-established, politically-connected businesses induce politicians to pass licensing laws that are specifically designed to stifle, and in many cases, to eliminate their competition.

REGULATIONS

There are laws to regulate where we can and cannot smoke, what drugs or herbs we are allowed to buy, what speed we can drive, who we can hire, the minimum we must pay them, what type of guns we can own, where we can take them, where we can and cannot protest, what personal items we can and cannot carry onto an airplane, and where we can and cannot pray.

Big government is involved in our lives from the moment we are born (birth certificates, mandated inoculations, Social Security numbers issued) until the time we die (burial regulations, death certificates, inheritance taxes...). From the womb to the tomb, it intrudes into our most private and personal affairs.

The food we eat, the drugs we take, the water and milk we drink, the schools we attend, the weapons we own, the radios we listen to, the movies and TVs we watch, even the air we breathe are all regulated by government.

Government regulations have given us toilets that don't flush properly, expensive light bulbs that are dangerous, and health-care that most people can't afford. It is clear that our freedoms are decreasing in direct proportion to increasing government regulations.

"According to the Office of the Federal Register, in 1998, the Code of Federal Regulations, the official listing of all regulations in effect, contained a total of 134,723 pages in 201 volumes, that claimed 19 feet of shelf space...The General Accountability Office (GAO) reports that in the four fiscal years from 1996 to 1999, a total of 15,286 new federal regulations went into effect. Of these, 222 were classified as 'major' rules, each one having an annual effect on the economy of at least $100 million...While they (the General Accounting Office) call the process 'rule-making', the regulatory agencies create and enforce 'rules' that are truly laws, many with the potential to profoundly affect the lives and livelyhoods of millions of Americans." [24]

To say that excessive government regulations are costly and a tremendous drag on the economy would be an understatement indeed.

"A new report on the government's regulatory actions was released just before Thanksgiving, and it contains more than 3,300 rules which the Competitive Enterprise Institute (CEI) estimates will, together with other regulations, cost more than $1.8 trillion to implement on an annual basis." [25]

Our government continues to grow bigger and bigger, creating more and more programs and agencies that create more and more regulations. All these programs and agencies require enormous sums of money which are funded through taxes. Why do we put up with this?

---

[24] Robert Longley, "About Guide to U.S. Government". *About.com.us government info.*

[25] Shannon Brean, "Regulation Nation: Gov't. Regs. Estimated to Pound Private Sector with $1.8T in Costs", *FoxNews.com,* 12-6-13.

Will there ever be a time when we, like our founding fathers, say "Enough is enough!"? Will we reach a tipping point where we refuse to comply with confiscatory taxing?

> "It [government] increasingly intrudes upon individual freedom. The more the government regulates, the less room is left for individual freedom. And as government grows, it requires more and more taxes. Taking all taxes together, federal, state and local, the average citizen pays approximately 42 percent of his income in taxes. That means for the first five months of every year, he works not for himself but for the government." [26]

---

[26] John Eidsmoe. *God and Caesar, Biblical Faith and Political Action,* Wipf & Stock Publishers, p. 89.

CHAPTER 3

WHY BIGGER GOVERNMENT?

You would think everyone would want less government in order to enjoy the freedom and blessings Dr. Ramsay described in his oration. But you'd be wrong. Actually, there are several reasons why some people desire big government even though it means less freedom and less privacy.

They like the government to solve their problems. Like it or not, our government has assumed the job of solving our problems even though it was never designed to do that. Government's purpose is to make sure the freedoms and rights of the people are protected so that they can solve their own problems. In fact, the less government does, the more freedom people have. Freedom is lost when government goes into the problem-solving business.

> "Throughout history, there is a constant and sorry trend of government attempting to fix a problem, inevitably exacerbating the problem, and ultimately violating personal freedoms in the process." [27]

Pastor R.B. Thieme Jr. certainly understood this principle and he faithfully taught it to his congregation during his fifty-one year ministry by stating the problem:

> "Our government is filled with false opinion as to what constitutes legislation and how legislation can or cannot solve human problems. No human problems

---

[27] Judge Andrew P. Napolitano, *It Is Dangerous To Be Right When the Government Is Wrong*, p. 63.

are ever solved by intrusion upon privacy and freedom. Our Government has a false opinion that they can legislate answers to the problems of life. They cannot. Their purpose is to protect the rights, the privacy, and the freedom of the individual, not to destroy it. Yet, their legislation now is destructive." [28]

Even though some in government want to help the plight of those who are in need, they blunder when they go beyond the Constitution and create programs.

But some may ask, "What about the poor, the needy, and the infirm?" How can they receive proper care without government support and programs? It's instructive to answer this question with a question, Who took care of the needy before there were welfare programs or government support? Family, friends, churches, and charitable organizations cared for them more quickly and more efficiently than government ever has.

Government programs are costly and extremely inefficient because they are run by bureaucrats who require a mountain of time-consuming forms and documents to be filled out. Government is a monopoly that has no competition from the private sector, so it has no incentive to be more efficient or to improve its services.

"There is a basic principle that many forget... the larger the unit of government, the more it will cost, the slower it will move, and the less it will do what the citizens expect." [29]

---

[28] R.B. Thieme Jr, *Unpublished. Notes,* "2 Thess. 2:11".

[29] Arthur R. Thompson, "The Problem with Local Regionalization", *The JBS Bulletin,* June 2012, No. 637, p. 1.

There are hundreds of examples of bloated and extremely inefficient government programs replete with waste and fraud. The following few examples were taken from www.heritage.org research reports:

"The Securities and Exchange Commission spent **$3.9 million** rearranging desks and offices at its Washington, D.C., headquarters."

"Health care fraud is estimated to cost taxpayers more than **$60 billion** annually."

"A Department of Agriculture report concedes that much of the **$2.5 billion** in 'stimulus' funding for broadband Internet will be wasted."

"The state of Washington sent $1 food stamp checks to 250,000 households in order to raise state caseload figures and trigger **$43 million** in additional federal funds."

Washington is always ready to come up with a new government solution for every problem, need, conflict or difficulty that arises. And if a new program bombs as most of them do, the government just throws more money at it so the program gets bigger and problems get worse Nothing attracts government money more than failure.

We don't need another government program! If the free enterprise system was allowed to work unfettered as it once did, the ingenuity generated from the natural competitive spirit in the private sector would rise back up where we'd find answers to help us solve our own problems.

> "It is definitely time to shed the naïve idea that the modern humanistic state exists to perpetuate good government. It is there to perpetuate itself at all costs. *No bureaucracy works itself out of a job.*" [30]

So why would anyone want to perpetuate horribly inefficient and inordinately expensive government programs that stifle free enterprise? And why do we allow the government to take over our job of taking care of ourselves? Here are a few of the reasons:

1. SECURITY

> *And my God will supply all your needs according to His riches in glory in Christ Jesus.* **Philippians 4:19**

People need to feel secure and safe, but since they no longer trust God to supply their needs, they have turned to government. Losing a job, money, health, home, or possessions can be traumatic, so when the government steps forward and offers security, many people are willing to accept the offer. They don't realize that there is a great price to be paid when they rely on government for security.

The first price is the loss of privacy.

Privacy is an integral part of our freedom. In fact, without privacy, there is no freedom. So here we are with a government that is determined to know absolutely everything about us. Recently it was discovered that the NSA, FBI, and CIA have been spying on us for many years, collecting and storing our personal and private information.

---

[30] John H. Whitehead; "Christian Resistance In the Face of State Interference", *Christianity and Civilization,* Geneva Divinity School, p. 1. [emphasis in original]

And now we are told that it was done for our own good in order to keep us safe and that we should trust them not to use that information against us, even though it was collected without our permission and without our knowledge. Are Americans really gullible enough to believe that?

> "It seems that there is virtually no intrusion into our personal lives and liberties so egregious that the American people will not support it, if it is presented as a way of making them more 'secure'... Today, the vast majority of the American people don't think twice about the government tracking them and listening to them through their cell phones, spying on their financial transactions, recording their phone conversations, reading their emails, scanning the data on their computers, setting up ubiquitous checkpoints on highways, and now sending drones over their homes and neighborhoods." [31]

To sacrifice freedom and privacy for nothing more than the empty promises of security from government is a very foolish and devastating trade. Once freedom and privacy are lost, they are extremely hard to get back.

When we are complacent, we tend to think life will continue as it always has and that there is no reason to believe that anything will significantly change. It is this thinking that lulls people into a false sense of security. We don't see the danger of being enslaved, especially since government subjugation sneaks up on us incrementally, a little bit at a time. If we don't wake up soon, it will be too late to do anything about it.

---

[31] Chuck Baldwin Live Blog, *Americans Putting the Noose Around Their Own Necks,* October 4, 2012.

2. MONEY

For the love of money is a root of all kinds of evil, for which some have strayed from the faith in their greediness, and pierced themselves through with many sorrows. **1 Timothy 6:10**

Multitudes of people are depending on government handouts now. Naturally, they want to keep those checks coming even though the government must go deeper in debt to support them. These millions on welfare and food stamps would certainly be unhappy if government started operating under its Constitutional restraints.

Universities that receive government grants, students who receive government loans, farmers and businesses who receive government subsidies have an interest in keeping the status quo. Why would farmers who get paid by the government for not planting a particular crop want to change that?

And why would people in foreign countries who receive billions in foreign aid want to stop our unconstitutional practice of giving them money? Or why would illegal aliens receiving billions in benefits want policies to change?

It is natural for people to take advantage of the financial aid offered to them by the government, but it is the politicians who are responsible for our national financial calamity for passing laws that take money from those who earn it and give it to those who don't.

Politicians, judges, bureaucrats, lobbyists, and a multitude of lawyers work for the government. The bigger the government, the greater their job security is because it generates greater demand for those types of jobs. This is true for thousands of government workers employed in useless, bloated government departments and agencies. They want to keep their jobs, so they have no interest in cutting down the size of government.

3. IGNORANCE

It is not good for a person to be without knowledge.
Proverbs 19:2

"Educate and inform the whole mass of the people... They are the only sure reliance for the preservation of our liberty."
~ Thomas Jefferson ~

People must stay informed and know their rights if they expect to remain free and independent. Those who know little or nothing about the Bible or the Constitution lack the knowledge required to hold their leaders accountable and consequently, lack the moral courage to challenge their unconstitutional actions.

The following quotes are taken from well-known men who understood the importance of being informed.

"It is impossible to enslave mentally or socially a Bible-reading people. The principles of the Bible are the groundwork of human freedom."
~ Horace Greeley ~

"If a nation expects to be ignorant and free, it expects what never was and will never be."
~Thomas Jefferson ~

"A nation of well-informed men who have been taught to know and prize the rights which God has

given them cannot be enslaved. It is in the region of ignorance that tyranny begins."
~ Benjamin Franklin ~

The schedule of average Americans today is so full and busy just trying to make a living and rearing their children that they have little time for anything else. They rarely read or do any research that would enable them to distinguish the truth from the misinformation circulating in the workplace and community. If they would only read more and choose good conservative books and internet articles, they would be better equipped to deal with the outright lies they hear from the media.

Average Americans don't know what the Constitution says and are not concerned enough to find out, so they remain naïve and susceptible to unscrupulous leaders who quickly take advantage of them. We live in evil times and cannot afford to stick our heads in the sand and remain oblivious to the machinations of malevolent, power-hungry men and women.

The Bible contains many passages that emphasize the importance of having wisdom and discernment, and staying alert.

> *For wisdom will enter your heart and knowledge will be pleasant to your soul; 11) discretion will guard you, understanding will watch over you, 12) to deliver you from the way of evil, from the man who speaks perverse things.* **Proverbs 2:10-12**
>
> *...be shrewd as serpents and innocent as doves.* **Matthew 10:16**

Ignorance is definitely one of the greatest enemies of freedom.

Those who have knowledge of the Bible and the Bill of Rights remain free, but those who choose to remain ignorant will be destroyed.

> *My people are destroyed for lack of knowledge.* **Hosea 4:6**
>
> *A prudent person foresees danger and takes precautions. The simpleton goes blindly on and suffers the consequences.* **Proverbs 22:3**
>
> *Through knowledge, the righteous will be delivered.* **Proverbs 11:9**

Wisdom is acquired from the Bible and it is the great friend of freedom. It not only empowers but it also protects.

> *A wise man is strong, and a man of knowledge increases power.* **Proverbs 24:5**

4. MANIPULATION

> *The thoughts of the righteous are just, but the counsels of the wicked are deceitful. 6) The words of the wicked lie in wait for blood, but the mouth of the upright will deliver them.* **Proverbs 12:5-6**

Today, a sizeable percentage of our population believes they hear reliable information on various news broadcasts from the mainstream media. They seem to be unaware of the propaganda and hype designed to lure listeners towards their politically correct viewpoint. Are people really unaware that the 6:00 o'clock news filters out what they don't want us to see and "spins" what we do see? People are not being informed; they are being programmed.

From sports programming to reality shows, from the Olympics to the Oscars, the distractions are endless and continue to captivate our attention. One might compare them to a sleight-of-hand on a grand scale.

There is nothing wrong with enjoying programs or following sports, but when you know every detail about your favorite sports team or reality show, but have no clue what your elected officials are up to, you are asking for trouble. When someone says they religiously follow a particular football team or TV program, they're not exaggerating. It has become their religion.

> "The imperial method employed for controlling the urban crowds, 'bread and circuses', was already nothing new in Augustus' time, but it was he who developed its application systematically... The people were kept happy [and distracted], and Augustus showed his successors how this could be done." [32]

> "How fortunate for leaders that men do not think."
> ~ Adolf Hitler ~

Wait a minute! Read that again. Hitler benefitted from the ignorance of his own people and so does every other would-be dictator whether in Germany or America. TV programming is relentless in its effort to dumb-down people and divert their attention away from the shenanigans of corrupt, governing officials.

Unscrupulous politicians passed the infamous Federal Reserve Act on December 23, 1913, two days before Christmas. They counted on the public being too involved in holiday festivities to notice their nefarious activities going on behind the scenes.

---

[32] Michael Grant, *The Twelve Caesars,* (1975), p. 75.

People are not so easily fooled who know our nation's history and the immutable principles of freedom found in the Word of God. Those who study God's Word can think for themselves and are less apt to be led around like sheep because they have developed discernment and wisdom. It's not easy to manipulate, use, or abuse people who know their rights and the laws of God that protect them.

5. LAZINESS

The soul of the sluggard craves and gets nothing, but the soul of the diligent is made fat. **Proverbs 13:4**

If anyone will not work, neither shall he eat. **2 Thess. 3:10**

Why should welfare recipients take care of their own financial responsibilities when the government has promised to meet their every need from the cradle to the grave? Many see government as their benevolent benefactor and feel obliged to support it and submit to it since it provides so much aid.

The desire of the sluggard puts him to death, for his hands refuse to work. **Proverbs 21:25**

The hand of the diligent will rule, but the lazy man will be put to forced labor. **Proverbs 12:24**

The following quote came from an Irish public servant named John Philpot Curran (1750-1817):

"It is the common fate of the indolent [lazy] to see their rights become a prey to the active."

Freedom is not free; it requires maintenance, vigilance, self-reliance, sacrifice, and courage, all of which are totally unappealing to those who are apathetic sluggards. It is much easier to simply ignore all the instances of oppression and pretend that all is well.

6. DEPENDENCE

Thus says the LORD: "Cursed is the man who trusts in man and makes flesh his strength." **Jeremiah 17:5**

We would do well to heed the warning from Henry Ford:

> "Any man who thinks he can be happy and prosperous by letting the government take care of him better take a closer look at the American Indian."

Unfortunately, the attitude of dependency prevails throughout our land. Many are more concerned about securing their spot at the federal feed trough than they are about being free and independent. Sacrificing freedom for security has always been a ruinous trade.

The policies and programs of our government foster an attitude of dependency, encourages laziness, and stifles ambition and goal-setting. They have destroyed the self-respect, dignity, and dreams of millions who now depend on them to take care of them. The independent, self-reliant spirit that Americans were known for has all but vanished.

During the "American War for Independence", George Bancroft demonstrated how important independence is and how he considered dependence to be an outward display of weakness and folly.

> "Each man's interests are safest in his own keeping, so

in like manner, the interests of the people can best be guarded by themselves...." [33]

Benjamin Franklin weighed in on the issue of dependence when he said, "They that can give up essential liberty to purchase a little temporary safety deserve neither liberty nor safety."

One of the worst things that can happen to free people is to grow so accustomed to the incremental encroachments on their God-given rights that they don't even notice that they're no longer free.

> "None are more hopelessly enslaved than those who falsely believe they are free."
> ~Goethe~

Many complain when they think the government isn't doing enough or not providing solutions fast enough, so they ask, "Why doesn't government do something about this?" They see nothing wrong with big government solving their problems because it is larger than any private business or industry and it has hundreds of programs already in place to help people. What's wrong with that?

According to the tenth article of the Bill of Rights, the federal government has no Constitutional authority to solve our problems or implement any programs for that purpose.

Do people not realize that a government big enough to give them all they want is also a government big enough to take away all they have?

---

[33] D Barton, *Celebrate Liberty!* (2003). *Famous Patriotic Speeches & Sermons* (84–85). Aledo, TX: Wall Builders Press.

7. FEAR

In God I have put my trust; I will not be afraid. What can man do to me? **Psalm 56:11**

It's very sad that so many Americans fear their own government and lack the courage and resolve to resist its tyrannical acts. It takes guts and tenacity to hold government officials accountable. It's much easier and safer to take the line of least resistance and do nothing to stop them. Doing nothing is usually the worst option when facing trouble.

There comes a time when tolerance is not a virtue and to do nothing is a sin.

Therefore, to one who knows the right thing to do and does not do it, to him it is sin. **James 4:17**

It is important that we refuse to suffer injustice from politicians who ignore the limitations placed on them by God and our founding documents.

Who encourages Americans to defend their God-given rights? Who inspires and teaches us from the Scriptures how God loves to exalt us when we take a stand for righteousness and justice? Who is telling us that we don't have to submit to government unconditionally? Certainly not our pastors.

Most pastors today avoid addressing issues concerning individual rights and government abuse because they are afraid someone might be offended, accuse them of being too political or think they are straying from what the Bible teaches. They have failed in their mission to be the watchmen on the wall who warn of encroaching danger.

They tell their congregations, "Don't rock the boat", "Don't make waves", "You can't fight city hall", and "Just go along to get along so there won't be any trouble."

But it wasn't that way when our country was founded. Back then, strong and courageous pastors taught Scriptures that instructed, encouraged, and emboldened their congregations to take back their freedoms.

> "The pulpit was the most powerful single force in America for the creation and control of public opinion." [34]

The people of the thirteen American Colonies paid a great price to secure the wonderful blessings that Dr. Ramsay described in his oration. Many of them were brutalized by British troops, their homes were burned, their belongings were stolen, they suffered inhumane treatment in prisons, and many were killed. They were willing to pay that high price because they had the courage of their convictions.

The Scriptures encourage us to have courage and not to be afraid:

The LORD is my light and my salvation; whom shall I fear? The LORD is the strength of my life; of whom shall I be afraid? **Psalm 27:1**

The fear of man brings a snare, but he who trusts in the LORD will be exalted. **Proverbs 29:25**

---

[34] Deward F. Humphrey, *Nationalism and Religion in America, 1774-1789* (1924) p. 24.

> *Be strong, and let your heart take courage, all you who hope in the LORD.* **Psalm 31:24**

Samuel Adams had this to say to people who were afraid to stand up for their God-given rights: "If ye love wealth greater than liberty, the tranquility of servitude greater than the animating contest for freedom, go home and leave us in peace. We seek not your council, nor your arms. Crouch down and lick the hand that feeds you; and may posterity forget that ye were our countrymen."

We must not be afraid to stand for what is right, regardless of the cost. John Philpot Curran understood this when he said, "Assassinate me you may; intimidate me you cannot." (1750-1817)

8. INDIFFERENCE

> *So then, while we have opportunity, let us do good to all people, and especially to those who are of the household of the faith.* **Galatians 6:10**

> *...so that there may be no division in the body, but the members may have mutual concern for one another.* **1 Corinthians 12:25***(NET)*

Often people are indifferent because they have given up any hope that anything can be done to change a situation. Men like Rev. John Witherspoon understood the danger of apathy and complacency. As a Convention delegate from the colony of New Jersey, he argued in favor of separation from England, declaring:

> "Gentlemen, New Jersey is ready to vote for independence. In our judgment, the country is not only ripe for independence, but we are in danger of

becoming rotten for the want of it, if we delay any longer!" [35]

Suffering humiliation without any effort to resist a bully or oppressive government that victimizes you and your family is dishonorable and displeasing to God. He expects us to stand for truth and righteousness against tyrants and to protect those who are innocent.

> *Be strong, and let us show ourselves courageous for the sake of our people and for the cities of our God; and may the LORD do what is good in His sight.* **2 Samuel 10:12**

> *Be on the alert, stand firm in the faith, act like men, be strong.* **1 Corinthians 16:13**

> *...for time will fail me if I tell of Gideon, Barak, Samson, Jephthah, of David and Samuel and the prophets, 33) who by faith conquered kingdoms, performed acts of righteousness.* **Hebrews 11:32-33**

Some Christians believe that their sole responsibility to the state is to pray for it and obey it. They think that anything more would demonstrate a lack of faith in God to ultimately handle the situation. On the contrary, it requires a great deal of faith to stand against wickedness and tyranny.

Ever since Adam's fall, man has lived in a fallen world where evil abounds, and that is not going to change until Christ returns to set up His kingdom. But does that mean God wants us to submit to evil until Christ returns? Absolutely not!

---

[35] Witherspoon, John. *Edward Frank Humphrey, Nationalism and Religion* (Boston: Chipman Law Publishing Co., 1924), p. 85. Peter Marshall and David Manuel, *The Glory of America* (Bloomington, MN: Garborg's Heart' N Home, Inc., 1991), 2.5.

How can Christians be the light of the world God calls them to be in Matt. 5:14 if they are required to yield to darkness?

There are Christians who would never approve of resisting governing officials for any reason. They believe it's OK to vote but think it would be biblically incorrect to seek political office, get involved in political parties, campaign for political causes, or write letters to Congress. However, common sense and experience has taught us that Edmond Burke's famous quote is true:

"Evil prospers when good men do nothing."

Laura Hollis is a law professor at Notre Dame who certainly understands the quote above. She wrote the following in the Town Hall Magazine:

"The President, Nancy Pelosi and Harry Reid (with no small help from Justice John Roberts) take away our health care, and we allow it. They take away our insurance, and we allow it. They take away our doctors, and we allow it. They charge us thousands of dollars more a year, and we allow it. They make legal products illegal, and we allow it. They cripple our businesses, and we allow it. They announce by fiat that we must ignore our most deeply held beliefs – and we allow it. Where is your spine, America?

"Yes, I know people are complaining...So what? People in the Soviet Union complained. People in Cuba complain. People in China complain (quietly). Complaining isn't the same thing as doing anything about it. In fact, much of the complaining that we hear sounds like resignation: Wow. This sucks. Oh well, this is the way things are. Too bad." [36]

---

[36] Laura Hollis, *Town Hall Magazine*, Jan. 28, 2014; She is lawyer and Business Law Professor, University of Notre Dame.

A good biblical example of someone who did nothing about evil was Abraham's nephew, Lot. He was a believer who desired the prosperous life of the big city of Sodom although he was tormented by the sexually perverse society there, 2 Peter 2:8-9. The Scriptures do not mention even one thing Lot said or did to stem the tide of the evil in Sodom, so it continued to degenerate unabated until God finally had to destroy it, Gen. 19:13.

> "Our problem today is not so much the noise of the bad people as the silence from the good people." [37]

Silence in the face of evil is evil.

Dietrich Bonhoeffer was a German Lutheran pastor, theologian, dissident anti-Nazi, and founding member of the Confessing Church. His writings on Christianity's role in the secular world have become widely known. He said, "Silence in the face of evil is itself evil: God will not hold us guiltless. Not to speak is to speak. Not to act is to act." [38]

Reverend Martin Niemoeller was another pastor in Germany during World War II that warned against the danger of being indifferent.

> "In Germany, the Nazis first came for the communists, and I didn't speak up because I wasn't a communist. Then they came for the Jews, and I didn't speak up because I wasn't a Jew. Then they came for the trade unionists, and I didn't speak up because I wasn't a trade unionist. Then they came for the Catholics, but I didn't speak up because I was a protestant. Then they

---

[37] Tom Anderson, *Silence Is Not Golden, It's Yellow,* Western Islands, p. 64.

[38] International Bonhoeffer Society; June 22, 2009, LQ Cincinnatus.

came for me, and by that time, there was no one left to speak for me." [39]

The writer of *Vindiciae (p. 196)* gave advice that modern-day Americans might well heed. He warned: "A tyrant the more he is tolerated, the more he becomes intolerable."

Those who recognize that man is a fallen creature with an inherent sin nature would have a hard time disagreeing with Daniel Webster's famous quote: "God grants liberty only to those who love it and are always ready to guard and defend it."

> "Of all people in the world, Christians cannot sit back passively as evil men distort God's ministry on earth, excusing their apathy of non-resistance by laying the blame solely on those evil people who are performing the injustice." [40]

John H. Armstrong said the following in an article entitled, *"Common Grace: A Not So Common Matter"* from volume 3 of his writings called *Reformation and Revival*:

> "...We should concern ourselves still with this present world, its politics, art, music, economics, literature, science and general advancement. We do not expect to 'Christianize the world or its culture'. We know better, as we are realists. But as much as we are realists we are not pessimists either. We will stand against evil in this world, both personally and corporately.

---

[39] From a speech given by Niemöller on January 6, 1946, to the representatives of the Confessing Church in Frankfurt.

[40] Baldwin and Chuck Baldwin, *Romans 13, The True Meaning of Submission,* by Timothy, p. 134.

"We will strive to redress wrongs and to establish justice. We will seek to attack poverty, both privately and corporately, because it enslaves and destroys. But we will do all this, realizing that the church's mission is to 'preach Jesus Christ and Him crucified', not to establish a Christian government or political party." [41]

Those who willingly submit to tyranny because it offers them security, because it benefits them financially, because they are ignorant, because they're lazy, because they are afraid, or because they are indifferent, will eventually become slaves of the State. They will lose their honor, their freedom, their privacy, their money, their property, and could possibly even lose their lives.

Apparently, a large number of Americans are either unaware of this danger or are aware but are unwilling or afraid to challenge the status quo. So they do nothing, foolishly hoping that things will eventually get better.

We are doomed if we continue to depend on government to solve our problems. We must realize,

**GOVERNMENT IS NOT THE SOLUTION;
IT IS THE PROBLEM!**

---

[41] Carol Stream, Vol. 3: *Reformation and Revival*. 1994 (1) (116 Illinois: Reformation and Revival Ministries).

HERE IS THE MAIN QUESTION:

What are Christians to do about a government that ignores the Constitution, tramples on their rights, and invades their privacy?

Much rests upon your answer.

THREE VIEWPOINTS

Viewpoint 1
Some believe God has given unlimited authority to those who govern and we are to submit to them unconditionally without question. They believe we should obey every law regardless of how odious, oppressive, or immoral it may be.

Viewpoint 2
Others believe God limits the authority of those who rule when, and only when, it interferes with their religious beliefs and/or traditions. They would resist in matters of faith but not in matters of freedom.

Viewpoint 3
This viewpoint holds that God limits the authority of those who govern, not only in matters of faith, but also in matters of freedom. They believe we are to submit to legitimate authority but not to tyranny.

CHAPTER 4

VIEWPOINT 1

Unlimited Authority

Government's authority is unlimited and requires unconditional submission

"My country, right or wrong" is the mindset of those who support this viewpoint. It doesn't matter what their government does, they will support it in order to show allegiance to their country. If someone complains about a law, they will tell him, "You might not like it, but it's the law!" meaning every law must be obeyed without question.

This is the least rational of the three viewpoints. But most people who hold to this view would also have to agree that authority is limited in every other area of life. So why not in this one?

Parental authority is limited. Parents are not authorized to abuse their children. A husband's authority is limited. He is not allowed to abuse his wife. A pastor's authority is limited. He cannot force members of his congregation to come to church or to abide by his teaching. A boss's authority is limited. He cannot maltreat his employees or interfere with their private lives. A teacher's authority is limited. He or she cannot maltreat students or interfere in their family matters.

Chuck and Timothy Baldwin ask the obvious question of those who hold to government's unlimited authority viewpoint. "The scriptural principle that governs a citizen's submission to his civil authorities is the same principle that governs his or her submission to any other authority. Why is it only to civil authorities that Christians must give absolute and total submission?" [42]

You will not find an answer to this question in the Bible or in the Constitution because it is based on the false premise that citizens must render unconditional submission to the State. People have been programmed and propagandized into believing that we are to submit immediately and without question to civil authorities.

IS UNLIMITED AUTHORITY REASONABLE?

Does it sound reasonable that God would give some men unlimited authority over other men? If one has unlimited authority, he is answerable to no one, not even to God!

God is Sovereign and is the ultimate authority over the universe, but does this mean that His authority is unlimited and He can do anything?

The answer is "No" because there is a difference between having *ultimate authority* and having *unlimited authority*. God's authority is limited by the attributes of His own perfect character. His Sovereignty must harmonize with His Love, Righteousness, Justice, Veracity, Immutability, Omniscience, and Omnipotence.

---

[42] Timothy Baldwin and Chuck Baldwin, *Romans 13, The True Meaning of Submission,* p. 12.

God is sovereign but He cannot lie because perfect veracity (truthfulness) is part of His essence. He has never said anything that is not true. He cannot be unjust or unfair or do anything wrong because He is perfectly just and right about absolutely everything. He cannot be unloving in any way because He is perfect Love.

So, if perfect God does not possess unlimited authority, how could He delegate it to imperfect man? And why would He, even if He could? He knows that unstable, sinful, fallen man would use it to abuse and subjugate others.

Frederic Bastiat (1801-1850) wrote about the dreadful position citizens are put in when their law-makers impose unjust and/or immoral laws on them.

> "It is impossible to introduce into society a greater change and a greater evil than this: the conversion of the law into an instrument of plunder. In the first place, it erases from everyone's conscience the distinction between justice and injustice. No society can exist unless the laws are respected to a certain degree. The safest way to make laws respected is to make them respectable. When law and morality contradict each other, the citizen has the cruel alternative of either losing his moral sense or losing his respect for the law. These two evils are of equal consequence, and it would be difficult for a person to choose between them." [43]

Government is not our ultimate authority, God is. And we are directly answerable to the Lord Jesus Christ, Acts 5:29, Col. 1:18.

---

[43] Frederic Bastiat, *The Law, 1998, The Foundation for Economic Education*, p. 8.

> "In whatever form government may be, higher powers are always 'under' or 'below' God and never possess God's approval when it contradicts the good purposes for which God ordained government." [44]

God is the "highest authority and power". All legitimate or lawful authority comes from Him and He delegates only limited authority to His civil servants. They are the "governing authorities" or "higher powers" mentioned in Romans 13 (KJV) who are servants of God and answerable to Him.

Romans 13:1-2 says that we are to submit to governing *authorities* [Gr. "*exousia*"], sometimes referred to as higher *powers* [Gr. "*exousia*"]. If that submission is based solely on the authority or power they possess, then it follows that we must submit to Satan as well because he too has authority and power [Gr. "*exousia*"].

> *You used to* [live] *in sin, just like the rest of the world, obeying the devil—the commander of the powers* [Gr. "*exousia*"] *in the unseen world. (NLT)*
> **Ephesians 2:2**

Furthermore, we are commanded to resist the devil.

> *Resist the devil and he will flee from you.*
> **James 4:7**

> *Do not give the devil an opportunity.*
> **Ephesians 4:27**

> *Stand firm against the schemes of the devil.*
> **Ephesians 6:11**

---

[44] Chuck and Timothy Baldwin, *Romans 13, the True Meaning of Submission*, 2011, p. 25.

Be of sober spirit, be on the alert. Your adversary, the devil, prowls around like a roaring lion, seeking someone to devour. 9) But resist him, firm in your faith.... **1 Peter 5:8-9**

Since God requires us to resist the devil, doesn't it make sense that He would require us to resist tyrants in government who act on Satan's behalf as his ministers? It is not wise to comply with the malevolent, evil dictates of the wicked. They should be rebuked and their dictates, rejected.

23) These also are sayings of the wise. To show partiality in judgment is not good. 24) He who says to the wicked, "You are righteous", peoples will curse him, nations will abhor him; 25) but to those who rebuke the wicked will have delight, and a good blessing will come upon them. **Proverbs 24:23-25**

Who will you obey? There is only room for one at the top. By definition, there can be only one sovereign. The question is, "Is it God or government?"

"Who is sovereign, and to whom is man responsible? This source of sovereignty is also the source of freedom. If sovereignty resides in God and is only held magisterially by men, then the basic responsibility of ruler and ruled is to God, who is also the source of freedom. But if sovereignty resides in the state, whether a monarchy or democracy, a man has no appeal beyond the law of the state, and no source of ethics apart from it." [45]

Would God give unlimited power to fallible men to rule

---

[45] Rousas John Rushdoony, *This Independent Republic*, Ross House Books, 1964, p. 14.

over us and then condemn us for resisting them when they abuse us? Does that sound like something a just and righteous God would do? Would a loving and an all-wise God give unlimited authority to men who have an inherent sin nature?

> "The usurpation of power and the abuse of power are not of God, for he is not the author of sin; but the power itself is." [46]

God has delegated authority to the state, but it is limited!

> "Caesar's authority is limited... When the state abandons its divine commission; it usurps God's authority and replaces Him in the life of a nation. Neither it nor its leaders answer any longer to God but proclaim themselves as lords of the citizenry. As the United States drifts from its Judeo-Christian heritage and as the state becomes ever more pervasive in American life, government could ultimately insist on full allegiance from the people, an allegiance belonging only to God. American government seems to have begun viewing itself as master, not servant. Agencies without any reference to God's laws, are seeking to regulate more and more spheres of public and private life; files of data on its citizens are expanding; and bureaucracy increasingly asserts its authority. While these trends may have begun with good intentions, they reflect a dangerous tendency to deny deity to the Creator and claim it for Uncle Sam... The state is a servant, not a sovereign." [47]

---

[46] Matthew Henry (1994) *Matthew Henry's Commentary on the Whole Bible: Complete and Unabridged in One Volume* (Rom. 13:1-6). Peabody: Hendrickson.

[47] H. Wayne House, *The Duty of Civil Disobedience to the Government: Contemporary Struggles Between Christians and the State*, p. 142-143.

DOES GOD REQUIRE SUBMISSION TO TYRANTS?

No. But some people believe we are required to submit unconditionally to officials based solely on their de facto rank or position in government. This thinking comes from the assumption that since God ordained government, He sanctions every action made by its civil servants including unjust and abusive ones. However, common sense dictates that this is absolutely false. God ordained government, but He never condones injustice, especially in government since those in government are to serve as His ministers of justice.

Why should we automatically assume that we must submit to those who abuse us simply because they wear a badge or have a title? How can anyone believe that our just and righteous God would condone their oppression and then require us to submit to it?

He would never require us to submit to evil men simply because they possess authority. Their position of authority does not justify their evil deeds. So the idea that God requires people to submit to leaders based solely on their title of authority is 100% false.

The argument that every person who holds de facto power is ordained of God is ludicrous. The fact that some use their authority to wield it over the lives and property of others does not mean that their behavior is sanctioned or ordained by God. He ordains government but *the behavior* of those in government determines whether they have or do not have God's endorsement.

Some believe we should submit to tyranny based on the Biblical principle that God sometimes uses tyrants to discipline a rebellious nation, and in that case, resisting the tyrant would be the same as resisting God.

While it is true that God sometimes uses the wicked to discipline a nation, it is a mistake to conclude that we are required to submit to their tyranny. God may use wicked rulers, but He never condones or approves of their behavior and eventually, He destroys them.

The old saying is true, "People get the government they deserve." Ignorant and apathetic people who are afraid to demand justice from their leaders have doomed themselves to suffer under the heavy hand of tyranny.

> "Now more than ever before, the people are responsible for the character of their Congress. If that body be ignorant, reckless and corrupt, it is because the people tolerate ignorance, recklessness and corruption."
> ~James A. Garfield~
> (20th president of the United States)

A government that is out of control is a fascist government. **Fascism** is described by Richard J. Maybury:

> "It is not only cruel, it has no objection to lies or contradictions. Since it assumes there is no law higher than the government's law, fascism requires total obedience to the state. It is nationalistic, hyper-patriotic, the ultimate in 'My country right or wrong'. Militaristic, it glorifies soldiers who are willing to go anywhere and fight anyone... Fascism says that government should do whatever appears necessary to serve its own interests." [48]

He gives an example of how much control a fascist government exerts over its citizens.

---

[48] Richard J. Maybury, *Ancient Rome, How It Affects You Today,* 2004, Bluestocking Press, pp 47-48, 53.

"Fascism assumes it has the right to intervene anywhere and control anything. Example: In 1994 Germany's Minister of Agriculture drafted a law requiring dog owners to spend two hours of 'quality time' daily with their dogs." [49]

Consider the German people during WW II. Who in his right mind would believe that God required him to obey Hitler's demands to turn Jews over to the Gestapo to be tortured and killed simply because he, their Führer, ordered it? God is perfectly just and the Jews are His chosen people. It is ludicrous to think that He would condone, much less demand, that German people obey such evil orders.

"Submission is due to all constitutional laws... Unlimited submission, however, is not due [owed] to government in a free state. There are certain boundaries beyond which submission cannot be justly required, nor is therefore due [owed]." [50]

The United States of America has a Constitution and a Bill of Rights that stand between "We the People" and tyrants. But those who do not know their rights or who refuse to demand that their rights be respected will suffer abuse.

"The advantage of a written constitution, considered as the original contract of society must immediately strike every reflecting mind; power when undefined, soon becomes unlimited... every man should know his own rights, it is also indispensably necessary that he should be able, on all occasions, to refer to them." [51]

---

[49] *Ibid* p. 54

[50] Minister John Tucker of Newbury, Mass. *Election Sermon, 1771.*

[51] George Tucker, *On the Study of Law,* p. 105.

SHOULD WE TRUST OUR GOVERNMENT?

It is better to trust in the LORD than to put confidence in princes. **Psalm 118:9**

It seems plausible that people should not submit unconditionally to a government they do not trust. Certainly those who gave us the Declaration of Independence, the Constitution, and the Bill of Rights did not trust government. They anticipated government overreach and abuse. These documents established a nation whose people valued liberty above all, so they included safeguards to protect the people from a government that might try to exceed its boundaries someday and abuse its power.

"In questions of power, then, let no more be heard of confidence in man, but bind him down from mischief by the chains of the Constitution."
~ Thomas Jefferson ~

Only the foolish or naive think kings and governments can be trusted to restrain themselves. People succumb to slavery by routinely allowing government officials to break their oaths of office without holding them accountable.

Rev. John Mayhew, one of the pastors during the War of Independence from England, said:

"History affords no example of any nation, country, or people, long free, who did not take some care of themselves and endeavor to guard and secure their own liberties. Power is of a grasping, encroaching nature, and operating according to mere will, whenever it meets with no balance, check control, or opposition of any kind." [52]

---

[52] Minister Jonathan Mayhew of Boston, *Sermon,* 1766.

Tyranny that develops incrementally over time is less likely to be resisted than when it comes suddenly or violently.

> "Civil tyranny is usually small at the beginning, like 'the drop in a bucket', till at length, like a mighty torrent, or the raging waves of the sea, it bears down all before it, and deluges whole countries and empires." [53]

Who would dispute that the encroachment of our government has been slow and methodical? Over the years, one infringement after another has diminished our freedoms at a rate that would not stir the people to action.

> "There are more instances of the abridgement of the freedom of the people by the gradual and silent encroachment of those in power, than by violent and sudden usurpation."
> ~James Madison ~

> "If the United States' president was to demand to be hailed as 'divine Caesar', and the state created an open religious cult like Roman state paganism, Americans in their vast majority would rebel. But as long as these claims come in quietly, and without fanfare, in the form of a shift in the basis of law and government, Christians may remain tranquil. While Christians are dormant, the pagan state continues to enlarge and consolidate its gains. If this continues for much longer, when Christians wake up, it will be too

---

[53] Jonathan Mayhew, 1749, to the Council and House of Representatives in Colonial New England. Dorothy Dimmick, "Why Study the Election Sermons of Our Founding Generation?" (San Francisco, CA: *The American Christian Prompter, Winter 1993*), Vol. 4, No. 2, p. 3.

late to do anything but suffer." [54]

Our federal government is divided into three branches to make sure that a balance of power is maintained. Each branch acts to keep the other two branches in check. However, that check and balance system has broken down. For example, consider the following excerpt from a news article by CBS News:

> "President Obama seems ready to work around Congress in 2014, telling reporters before his first Cabinet meeting of the year Tuesday that he stood ready to use two tools, a pen and a phone, to provide help for Americans. [He said] 'We are not just going to be waiting for legislation in order to make sure that we're providing Americans the kind of help that they need. I've got a pen, and I've got a phone. And I can use that pen to sign executive orders and take executive actions and administrative actions that move the ball forward ... I've got a phone that allows me to convene Americans from every walk of life ... to try to bring more and more Americans together around what I think is a unifying theme....'" [55]

This is possibly the most blatantly dictatorial statement made by any president, demonstrating his utter contempt for our Constitution and the **Rule of Law**. What colossal arrogance it takes to make such a statement.

---

[54] John H. Whitehead; "Christian Resistance In the Face of State Interference", *Christianity and Civilization,* Geneva Divinity School Press, 1983, p.3

[55] Rebecca Kaplan, "Obama: I will use my phone and pen to take on Congress", *CBSNEWS.COM,* January 14, 2014.

Any action taken by Congress or the Whitehouse, regardless of how obviously unconstitutional it is, is now being accepted, not only by most governors, State congressmen and senators, mayors, judges, and sheriffs, but also, and most disappointingly, by We the People.

Our Congress gave hundreds of billions of our tax dollars to banks that had recklessly gambled away huge sums of their investors' money. But when the people protested, Congressional leaders justified their nefarious act with the feeble excuse that the bailout was necessary because things would get worse if the banks were not saved.

> "Necessity is the plea for every infringement of human freedom. It is the argument of tyrants; it is the creed of slaves."
> ~ William Pitt, Nov. 18, 1783 ~

So what happened to the top bank executives who recklessly ran their companies into the ground and then asked the government to save them? Were they fired? No. They received fat bonuses! No one in banking or in government was censured, punished, fired, or incarcerated.

But isn't our nation supposed to be governed by the **Rule of Law** as codified in the Constitution and Bill of Rights rather than the machinations of men?

We have tolerated this kind of reprehensible behavior from our legislators for so long that we now find ourselves at the edge of a financial cliff with our economy and healthcare about to plummet into utter chaos.

Government scandals have become so routine that people hardly pay any attention to them. The Benghazi scandal where our embassy was attacked by terrorists, and four Americans were killed, including the U.S. ambassador, has already been mentioned. Our military was ready to come to their aid but was told to stand down. The IRS scandal exposed the efforts of its agents to prevent certain non-profit organizations from receiving tax exempt status based solely on their political beliefs.

Most bills that our Congress passes are loaded with pork and enticements that help persuade its members to vote for them. So, most politicians just vote along party lines unless they are pressured to do otherwise by special interest groups or enticements in the bill.

These unconstitutional bills are usually hundreds and sometimes thousands of pages long. Sometimes Congress has less than an hour or two to read them before they vote, so they have no idea what is really in the bill. The ObamaCare law has 961 pages consisting of 2,163,744 words. The King James Version of the Bible contains 830,314 words. That makes Obama-Care regulations two and a half times longer than the Bible! This is ridiculous.

Statistics are found at: http://obamacarewatcher.org/articles/350

Now Americans are forced to buy government-mandated health insurance that most people don't like and can't afford.

Why are our leaders allowed to get by with disregarding the Constitution and the will of the people? The answer is obvious... because we allow it! Most politicians continue to get re-elected in spite of making a mockery of the Constitution they swore to uphold.

A man who makes a vow to the Lord or makes a pledge under oath must never break it. He must do exactly what he said he would do. **_Numbers 30:2_**

Make vows to the LORD your God and fulfill them. **_Psalm 76:11_**

SHOULD WE TRUST OUR JUDICIAL SYSTEM?

Over time, the U.S. Supreme Court and State Supreme Courts have slowly moved away from their constitutional framework of interpreting law towards an all-powerful court system where judges essentially act as legislators who create laws

The entire nation can now be bound by five Supreme Court judges who are appointed for life and who primarily base their decisions on precedents set by previous courts rather than the organic Constitution. If an earlier court made a mistake or used poor judgment in deciding a case, that precedent could be perpetuated on to later courts. It appears that this ideology has led the court away from its constitutional moorings over time and has broken down the separation of powers between the branches of government, thus allowing the court to exert much more power than the Constitution intended.

The "separation of powers" built into the Constitution to limit any branch of government from becoming too autonomous has, at times, been brazenly ignored by the courts. When courts go beyond their job of applying the law to a case and start imposing their own personal opinions on it, they actually are legislating law rather than interpreting law.

Only Congress has legislative power, Article 1 Section 1:

"All legislative powers herein granted shall be vested in the Congress of the United States..."

> "Courts go beyond 'plain meaning' interpretations, giving laws and even constitutional provisions new and innovative meanings that their authors never dreamed of... When the courts change the law at their own initiative, they are legislating, and the framers of the Constitution never intended them to do that." [56]

H. Wayne House is a distinguished research professor of theology, law, and culture at Faith Evangelical College and Seminary in Tacoma, Washington, and was formerly a professor of law at Trinity Law School and Trinity International University. Author and editor of several books, he says:

> "When Holmes and others applied an evolutionary perspective that law is in flux in society and is not founded on some absolute principles, judges began to make the laws. With this has come the usurpation by the court of functions of the other branches of government as well as the other jurisdictions God created in society. Jurisdictions that God has established, the state, the family, the church, and finally the individual, have been trampled on by the state, especially the courts, so that little has been untouched by their designs of social engineering." [57]

The following excerpt was taken from an article written by William Gray entitled, *"Is There Anything That Can*

---

[56] John Eidsmoe, *God and Caesar, Biblical Faith and Political Action,* Wipf and Stock Publishers, p. 90.

[57] H. Wayne House, (1999). *Christian Ministries and The Law:* Revised edition (26). Grand Rapids, Mich.: Kregel.

Be Done to Save the United States?" It can be found on the Worldview Weekend website, 8-29-12:

> "Ungodly arguments have resulted in ungodly decisions from ungodly jurists sitting on the U.S. Supreme Court who are not committed to godliness; this has resulted in the total abrogation of the constitutional principles established in the First Amendment to the United States Constitution and ratified by the states in 1787. They have done more to damage our nation than outside terrorists have ever thought about doing."

The more power the Court accrues to itself, the less freedom we have. The more power the government acquires, the less we have. The bigger it grows, the smaller, weaker, and more helpless we become. We will become inconsequential pawns to be used and abused by our gargantuan government if we remain compliant servants to those who are supposed to be serving us.

CONSTITUTIONAL AMENDMENTS THAT CRIPPLED AMERICA

It is public naivety that permits federal duplicity. The fact that the American people have been programmed by the media and duped by politicians for a long time is evident by the amendments that were added to the Constitution between 1868 and 1913 that fraudulently gave the federal government control over the States.

The fact that people allowed their State legislators to enact the disastrous 14th, 16th, 17th, and 18th Amendments to the Constitution demonstrates that people truly do get the government they deserve.

The 14th Amendment punished the South and destroyed state sovereignty.
The 16th Amendment instituted a progressive income tax.
The 17th Amendment allowed the election of Senators that effectively removed their accountability to the people.
The 18th Amendment instated prohibition.

THE 14TH AMENDMENT was no doubt the most dastardly and harmful of all. The scoundrels who created it were trying to turn the Constitution upside down by subordinating the sovereign States to the federal government that the States had created. The creator is always superior to what it creates.

Our country has never been the same since the infamous 14th Amendment because it gave the federal government carte' blanche power over the States.

"The political creature [the federal government] now has the temerity to dictate to its creators [the States]." [58]

Bear in mind that the original thirteen colonies designed the Constitution to keep our federal government in check by confining it to only well-defined and rigidly, specific, limited powers. They well knew the propensity of men to try to increase their power.

Also, "The Bill of Rights" (The first 10 Amendments) were added to make sure that the federal government respected the individual rights of the people.

The 9th Amendment declared that Americans have rights other than those listed in the Bill of Rights;

---

[58] *Christianity and Civilization,* Geneva Divinity School Press, 1983, p. 291.

"The enumeration in the Constitution, of certain rights, shall not be construed to deny or disparage others retained by the people."

The 10th Amendment recognizes the sovereignty of the States as well as the people. It keeps the federal government in check by giving it only the powers the Constitution specifically grants to it:

"The powers not delegated to the United States by the Constitution, nor prohibited by it to the States, are reserved to the States respectively, or to the people."

Some mistakenly think that the federal government can do anything it wants unless the Constitution prohibits it. Not so! It can do only what is specifically granted to it by the Constitution.

The federal government cannot lawfully exert any power unless it is explicitly conferred to it by the Constitution.

The wording in the Bill of Rights confirms the sovereignty of the States and the People over the federal government. It includes phrases that place prohibitions and demands on the federal government such as:

Article 1: "Congress shall make no law respecting an establishment of religion, or prohibiting the free exercise thereof…."

Article 2: "The right of the people to keep and bear arms shall not be infringed."

Article 3: "No soldier shall…be quartered in any house, without the consent of the Owner…."

Article 4: "The right of the people to be secure in their persons, houses, papers, and effects against unreasonable searches…shall not be violated…."

Article 5: "No person shall be held to answer for a capital, or infamous crime, unless on a presentment or indictment of a Grand Jury…."

Article 6: "In all criminal prosecutions, the accused shall enjoy the right to a speedy and public trial…."

Article 7: "the right of trial by jury shall be preserved…."

Article 8: "Excessive bail shall not be required…."

Article 9 & 10: (already addressed)

THE 14TH AMENDMENT:

Now notice how this wording changed absolutely everything.

Section 1, Second Sentence:

*"**No State** shall make or enforce any law which shall abridge the privileges or immunities of citizens of the United States, nor shall any State deprive any person of life, liberty, or property, without due process of law; nor deny the equal protection of the laws."*

Who enforces the stipulations of this amendment? The federal government, of course, in Section 5. So this amendment shifted sovereignty from the states to the federal government.

The 5th Amendment of the Bill of Rights, says, **"No person shall…be deprived of life, liberty, or property, without due process of law."**

Compare that to Section 1 of the 14th Amendment, ***"...nor shall any State deprive any person of life, liberty, or property, without due process of law".***

The wording is nearly identical, so what is the difference? The 5th Amendment limits the power of the federal government, whereas the 14th Amendment limits the power of the States. In effect, it repealed the Bill of Rights by giving the federal government unconstrained control over the once sovereign States. Now the Federal government tells the States what they can and cannot do which is exactly what our founding fathers tried to prevent. Today we have the tail wagging the dog.

We saw an example of this in 1994 in California's Proposition 187. This ballot initiative was overwhelmingly passed by the people denying "free", that is, taxpayer-funded, social services to illegal aliens. However, the will of the people was ignored by a federal judge who despotically prevented the implementation of the proposition in the name of the 14th Amendment. Now, the State of California is going bankrupt because our federal government forced it to give illegal aliens "free" education, "free" health-care, "free" hospital care, food stamps, and more.

In 2005, Texas voters overwhelmingly approved a Constitutional amendment that banned same-sex marriage. But in February of 2014, under the auspices of the 14th Amendment, a federal judge ruled that the Texas law was unconstitutional even though the U.S. Supreme Court has consistently recognized that States have the authority to define and regulate marriage. The case is under appeal at the time of this writing.

The 14th Amendment was passed in 1868 right after the Southern War for Independence, aka "The Civil War". The United States Congress used this amendment to punish the South and to place the States under the control of the federal government. If you find this hard to believe, read the 14th Amendment for yourself; it has five sections. **Section 1** has already been addressed.

Section 2 denied people the right to vote who participated in "rebellion". This, of course, referred to people in the South who were loyal to the Confederacy. Many Northerners treated Southerners as if they were criminals, guilty of insurrection and rebellion rather than the true patriots they were for fighting to retain the independence of their newly formed nation.

Section 3 says that anyone who had been loyal to the Confederacy and had once held an office in the U.S. government or military was no longer allowed to hold office in the United States.

Section 4 says that all debts owed by Southerners to those in the U.S. would remain in force and would not be questioned, but all debts owed to Southerners would be considered null and void.

Section 5 says that the Congress has the power to enforce the provisions of this amendment.

One reason martial law was imposed on the South after the war was to force them to ratify this abominable 14th Amendment. But even that was not enough to garner the votes required to ratify it; however it was enacted anyway which made it unlawful, and for all intents and purposes, null and void.

The first ten amendments to the Constitution are called the Bill of Rights because they represent a partial list of our God-given rights. They do not "give" us our rights; they only recognize some of the unalienable rights that God has given us. The government can never revoke any God-given rights, however, it can revoke the "privileges" and "immunities" mentioned in section 1 of the 14th Amendment. Whatever the government gives, it can also take away.

> "When government becomes the enemy of rights, it can be tossed out. Rights are permanent, inherent features of all humans; governments are devices that come and go according to the wishes of those who cede power to them. *Our natural rights cannot be changed or abolished, but governments can.*" [59]

Since the 10th Amendment was not revoked when the 14th Amendment was passed, a tension or conflict now exists between them. The 10th Amendment subordinates the federal government to the States, and the 14th subordinates the States to the federal government.

For a long time, our government has been ignoring the 10th and implementing the 14th. However, the States and the people can still use the 10th Amendment to nullify the unconstitutional acts of the federal government if they have the will and "know-how" to do it. Other Amendments that follow this one are nearly as bad.

> "The shift in power from the local and state level is plainly evident in all 50 States and in innumerable communities. It has been made possible by the unlimited

---

[59] Judge Andrew P. Napolitano, *It Is Dangerous To Be Right When the Government Is Wrong.* p.258-259 [emphasis in original]

taxing authority which the states unwisely granted the national government via the 16th Amendment in 1913. It was further enhanced by ratification of the 17th Amendment in the same year, which changed the election of senators by the various state legislatures to the people directly. This Amendment radically altered the original structure of the American Republic and practically eliminated the influence of the states as independent political entities in the national Congress. And, finally, the shift in power has been further solidified by the passage of the Federal Reserve Act [that also occurred in 1913] which created a central bank (the Federal Reserve System). This Act made it possible for the politicians and bureaucrats at the national level to engage in massive and continued deficit spending, thus insidiously transferring the control of privately created wealth from citizens into the hands of government rulers." [60]

Because the separation of powers between the three branches of the federal government has deteriorated over past decades, an even more aggressive attitude of power and superiority has been fostered in government officials.

GUILTY UNTIL PROVEN INNOCENT

Consider Gavin Siem who was traveling with his wife and three kids through New Mexico, eighty miles from the U.S./Mexican border, when he was stopped at a Homeland Security checkpoint. He asked if he was being detained and the officer said, "Yes". He asked on what grounds and was told that it was "on the basis of the Constitution". Unbelievable!

---

[60] Tom Rose, *Christianity and Civilization,* Geneva Divinity School Press, 1983, p. 292.

The officer had no legitimate reason or lawful grounds to stop Mr. Siem and his family since he had done nothing wrong or anything suspicious. The checkpoint was not set up to apprehend some criminal trying to flee the area. No, it was set up to indiscriminately stop and interrogate anyone driving in that area. It was a blatant infringement on Mr. Siem's right to travel freely. Of course the same old lame excuse for detaining and interrogating innocent Americans was used; "It is for your own good and safety." Balderdash! There is no legitimate excuse for disregarding the rights of the American people.

What is shocking is that U.S. government agents tried to defend their unlawful Gestapo behavior by saying the U.S. Constitution gave them such authority.

There was no reason to suspect this Caucasian family of illegally entering the U.S. or of doing anything wrong, so it was unlawful for the officers to stop and interrogate them. Mr. Siem refused to answer any of their questions and was eventually allowed to go on his way when they realized that he knew his rights and insisted that the officers respect them. The following is what he said after the incident.

> "In truth, rebelling against the rule of unjust law in order to oppose tyranny and immorality is by action to show utmost respect for law, order and justice. It is, and always has been, the epitome of human courage. Question and challenge government all the time — otherwise they will trample you every time." [61]

---

[61] Gavin Siem, "Detained Because of the Constitution?" Mike Maharrey, *Activism, Federal Power*, 6-4-1; http://blog.tenthamendmentcenter.com/2013/06/detained-because-of-the-constitution/

CHAPTER 5

VIEWPOINT 2

Limited Authority in Matters of Faith

This viewpoint recognizes that God limits governmental authority, but when it comes to matters of faith, one may rightly refuse to submit, and only in matters of faith. All other laws must be obeyed unless they threaten religious freedom.

For example, if the government passed a law that banned praying, going to church, or witnessing, Christians would have the biblical grounds to disregard it because they recognize that God's law is higher than man's law. It wouldn't matter who issued the law or where it came from; it should be ignored.

This is good and honorable, however obeying all other laws no matter how unconstitutional or unjust is not commanded in the Bible, and doing so is definitely not good or honorable. How can submitting to tyrants who abuse people be honoring to God? How could our just God command us to comply with an evil force that is destroying us? If we cooperate with evil, aren't we evil as well? Isn't that self-defeating?

GOING AGAINST OUR CONSCIENCE

It's a lot like knowing there's a dead fly in your soup and continuing to eat around it. You know that the dead fly (government injustice) is contaminating your soup (destroying your country), yet you continue to eat around it (submit to its abuse). By doing this, you are condoning, aiding and empowering the ever-growing tyranny that threatens us. How can this possibly be pleasing to God?

An evil ruler is the enemy of God and we are called to resist him, not to tolerate his lawlessness and abuse until our conscience can no longer take it. While Christians refuse to act, the entire country is drowning in the growing tsunami of tyranny. Now ask yourself:

Why would God allow us to disobey the government in matters of faith but not in matters of freedom or justice?

Wicked rulers who ignore civil liberties will eventually ignore religious liberties as well. You can count on it. We might as well kiss our freedom to worship goodbye if we keep failing to question or to resist politicians when they ignore our constitutional liberties.

Recently, an anti-discrimination law required a Christian florist to arrange floral displays for a same-sex wedding. It went against her conscience as well as her religious beliefs, so this courageous lady refused to obey it. She was tried, convicted, and fined for standing firm for her religious convictions.

How could this happen in America? The answer is simple: for far too long, people with Viewpoint #2 have been eating tyranny soup with a dead fly in it.

<u>Government considers silence to be consent</u>, so when there is no outcry from people when a florist is punished for expressing her religious beliefs, it emboldens the government to increase its oppression.

Like a roaring lion or a charging bear is a wicked ruler over a poor people. **Proverbs 28:15**

William Wilberforce said, "A private faith that does not act in the face of oppression is no faith at all."

> "Christians are not called by God to simply follow any given law because it is a law. Many laws are unjust and blatantly contrary to God's will. When they are not, however, we are not to resist these laws, to be rebels." [62]

Do people forfeit their God-given rights of freedom, privacy, and property when they become Christians? Not according to the Bible. Does the Bill of Rights protect everyone *except* Christians? Of course not. Therefore, they, like everyone else, have the Constitutional right to question, challenge or even disobey any laws that violate their rights.

> "The biblical view of government is that the state has only limited authority; there are many areas of human activity that are beyond the state's jurisdiction." [63]

THE RELIGION-GOVERNMENT LINK

Many Christians are indifferent to what goes on in Washington D.C. and fail to realize the connection between government and religion. They make it a point to avoid getting involved in political issues, then wonder why our society is degenerate and our freedoms are vanishing.

> "We are compelled to ask how is it that so much corruption, unlawfulness, evil acts, and government

---

[62] House, H. W. (1999). *Christian Ministries and The Law:* Revised edition (26). Grand Rapids, Mich.) p. 154.

[63] John Eidsmoe, *God and Caesar, Biblical Faith and Political Action;* Wipf and Stock Publishers, p. 84.

encroachment upon individual rights came about in the land. The old common law along with the rights of Life, Liberty, and Property has eroded away because the religion of the people has eroded away." [64]

If Christian voices continue to be silent in the political arena, Christians will lose their civil rights as well as their religious freedom.

"Many early English legal scholars such as John Locke had a profound impact on American thought. Locke claimed that the 'Word of God' as fundamental law which is to be utilized as 'a rule of righteousness to influence our lives' as a concrete means of checking arbitrary government." [65]

Can freedom be lost in the civil realm and still remain in the religious? Rev. John Witherspoon didn't think so. He championed against tyranny overruling conscience. He believed that religious liberty and civil liberty were inseparable and that the greatest service government could render to Christianity was, "to defend and secure rights of conscience in the most fair and impartial manner." He believed that religious liberty and civil liberty are inseparable.

"There is not a single instance in history, in which civil liberty was lost, and religious liberty preserved entire.... If therefore we yield up our temporal property, we at the same time deliver the conscience into bondage... [Governments are to] defend and secure

---

[64] Charles A. Weisman, *Life, Liberty, and Property*, Weisman Publications, 1997, p. 39.

[65] J.N. Figgis, *The Divine Right of Kings*, Cambridge, 1914, p. 311.

rights of conscience in the most equal and impartial manner." [66]

Most Christians remain silent about the tyranny they live under, foolishly believing that the government will leave them alone if they keep their mouths shut. They are under the illusion that our out-of-control government will not intrude into their church activities or in their efforts to give the gospel. But the government's tentacles have already wrapped around many 501c3 churches who asked to be incorporated by the government. Doing that is totally unnecessary since the 1st Amendment to the Constitution exempts churches from taxation. Furthermore, Jesus Christ is the Head of the church, not the State!

Christians are already being arrested for giving out the gospel on public street corners.

> "It is in the man of piety and inward principle, that we may expect to find the uncorrupted patriot, the useful citizen, and the invincible soldier. God grant that in America true religion and civil liberty may be inseparable and that the unjust attempts to destroy the one, may in the issue tend to [may result in] the support and the establishment of both." [67]

Yes, there is a direct link between freedom and religion. One affects the other. The spiritual vitality of the people determines what kind of government they

---

[66] John Eidsmoe, *Christianity and the Constitution—The Faith of Our Founding Fathers* (Grand Rapids, MI: Baker Book House, A Mott Media Book, 1987, 6th printing 1993), pp. 90-91.

[67] John Witherspoon, "The Dominion of Providence over the Passions of Men". May 17, 1776, Varnum Lansing Collins, President Witherspoon (*New York: Arno Press and The New York Times*, 1969), I: 197-98.

will accept. If pastors were diligent to teach the biblical limitations placed on government, Christians would be less likely to stand idly by while their leaders impose unlawful demands on them.

> "Freedom prospers when religion is vibrant and the Rule of Law under God is acknowledged."
> ~Ronald Regan~

We must realize that when public servants break their sworn oaths to protect and defend the Constitution, they become deceitful liars who have offended God and have violated our trust in them. When we fail to hold them accountable and continue to acquiesce to their unjust and unconstitutional laws, we lose the treasure trove of freedoms that God has graciously bestowed to us. So here is the question:

How can corrupt government officials be held accountable by Christians if the Bible requires Christians to obey every law and denies them the right to resist tyranny?

This is the critical question that must be answered by every Christian. And the answer is clear. If the Bible requires Christians to yield to injustice and forbids them to resist tyranny, then despots will prevail and freedom will be lost. Even the freedom to worship and to exercise our religious beliefs and traditions will disappear.

Samuel Adams, fourth Governor of Massachusetts, believed that tyranny and oppression wage war against their greatest foes: God, the Bible, and Christians.

> "As tyranny, oppression and usurpation become more commonplace in America and throughout the world,

one begins to see a war being silently yet diligently waged against God, the Bible, and Christianity. Like the political war against rights, the religious war is waged by our enemy with the aims of destroying the protections that guard the rights of Life, Liberty, and Property, as Samuel Adams stated in 1776." [68]

He understood the correlation between the spiritual vigor of people and their freedoms. He reminds us how the enemies of freedom continually work to eradicate our righteousness and trust in God.

"I fully agree in opinion with the celebrated Author, that Freedom or Slavery will prevail in a country according as the dispositions and manners of the people render them fit for one or the other; and I have long been convinced that our enemies have made it an object, to eradicate from the minds of the people a general sense of true religion and virtue, in hopes thereby the more easily to carry their point of enslaving them." [69]

There was another Adams, John Quincy, the sixth U.S. president, who also recognized the connection between religion, freedom, and government. "The highest glory of the American Revolution was this: It connected in one indissoluble bond, the principle of civil government with the principles of Christianity...." [70]

---

[68] John Quincy Adams, reprinted in J. Wingate Thornton, Vol. I, *Christian History of the Constitution* (1860), p. 372.

[69] Charles A. Weisman, *Life, Liberty, and Property,* by Weisman Publications 1997, p. 39. H. Cushing, *"The Writings of Samuel".*

[70] Adams, ed. N.Y., 1904, v.3, p. 286.

IS GOVERNMENT OR CONSCIENCE SUPERIOR?

Christians determine what is right and wrong from their Bibles and their conscience, both of which come from God. Both are superior to any man-made law. To go against conscience in order to obey a law is just wrong. It is going against the very thing God has given us to govern and guide our actions.

> "Must a citizen ever for a moment, or in the least degree, resign his conscience to the legislator? Why has every man a conscience, then? It is not desirable to cultivate a respect for the law, so much as for the right." Henry David Thoreau

It is true that there are a few people who have consciences so seared that it appears they have none at all.

> *But the Spirit explicitly says that in later times some will fall away from the faith, paying attention to deceitful spirits and doctrines of demons, 2) by means of the hypocrisy of liars seared in their own conscience as with a branding iron.* **1 Tim. 4:1-2**

There are people like Adolph Hitler who are not normal. They are exceedingly evil and appear to have no conscience, but they are the exception to the rule. That being said, God expects His Word, the Holy Spirit, and our conscience to guide us in making decisions that honor Him.

The English Puritan, William Perkins (1558-1602), wrote: "If it should fall out that men's law be made of things evil, and forbidden by God, then there is no bond of conscience at all; but contrariwise, *men are bound in conscience not to obey.*" [Emphasis added]

Did he say if men's laws are evil and go against our conscience, we are not bound to obey them? Yes, he did, so here is the question we need to ask ourselves once again: Why would we be allowed to act in accord with our conscience in matters of faith but not in matters of freedom and justice? Why would God give us a conscience to walk in the way of righteousness but at the same time, require us to submit to evil laws that go against our conscience?

> "All obedience to civil authority is limited by the higher allegiance due to God, its author. To imagine otherwise is to annihilate, by the law of God, its own authority and sanctions. All right subjection to civil rule regards it as the creature of God, but no more. It surely does not give it God's place. Indeed nothing can be more absurd than the notion that 'conscience', which also sees God as supreme in His claims and power, should for a moment substitute any 'lower law' for His. This would be to deny its own nature, to act in direct opposition to the very law of its being." [71]

James E. Woods Jr. agreed when he said the following in an article published in *The Ashland Theological Journal*:

> "Liberty, whether civil or religious, is freedom from the tyranny or the control of the state, the guaranteed right of dissent, and the freedom to obey one's own conscience in so far as it does not infringe upon the rights of others or threaten the stability of the social order... Certainly the totalitarian state is always a serious threat to the church and the cause of religion." [72]

---

[71] James M. Wilson, *The Establishment and Limits of Civil Government* (1883).

[72] James E. Wood Jr., "The American Tradition in Church and State", Vol. 5: *Ashland Theological Journal,* 1972 (10).

There are those who disagree with Mr. Woods. They believe just the opposite, that government authority is superior to the authority of individual conscience. John A. Witmer voiced this opinion favoring government superiority in an article entitled, *"A Man with Two Countries"*:

> "But no citizen, even the Christian, has the right to set himself up as legislature or as Supreme Court to decide which laws he will obey and which he will not obey whenever his worship of God or his proclamation of the gospel are not directly involved. When the individual's conscience has authority over law, then government by law is jeopardized." [73]

Some would tend to agree with Mr. Witmer that if people had the right to pick and choose which laws they would obey and which ones they wouldn't, they might feel free to disobey any law they didn't particularly like or they might choose to completely disregard all laws.

The fact is, anyone can do that now at any time, but Christians are bound by the Bible to obey higher powers (government officials) that fulfill their role as "ministers of God for good" and to obey all laws that are just and fair.

Since we live in a fallen world tainted by sin, we all must tolerate a certain amount of injustice. For instance, we encounter a bit of thoughtlessness, bad behavior, and injustice in all areas of life just about every day. The Word of God requires us to take this all in stride. We are not to retaliate but to treat others with kindness and love.

---

[73] John A. Witmer, "A Man with Two Countries", *Bibliotheca Sacra Volume 133* (133:532), p. 344-345; Dallas Theological Seminary. (1976; 2002). *Bibliotheca Sacra Volume 142*. 1985. Dallas, TX: Dallas Theological Seminary.

John Rawls rightly said: "Whether noncompliance is justified depends on the extent to which laws and institutions are unjust. Unjust laws do not all stand on a par, and the same is true of policies and institutions." [74]

The Declaration of Independence does a great job of addressing this.

> "Prudence, indeed, will dictate that governments long established should not be changed for light and transient causes; and accordingly all experience hath shewn that mankind are more disposed to suffer, while evils are sufferable than to right themselves by abolishing the form to which they are accustomed."

But, there comes a time when tolerance is no longer a virtue!

The Declaration puts it this way:

> "But when a long train of abuses and usurpations, pursuing invariably the same object evinces a design to reduce them under absolute despotism, it is their right, it is their duty, to throw off such a government, and to provide new guards for their future security."

Mr. Witmer's article mistakenly elevated government mandates above individual conscience except in instances where witnessing or worship is involved. Apart from these two issues, he would have us believe that we must ignore our conscience when the state requires us to do something against our will. It would appear that Mr. Witmer believes citizens are not competent to determine for themselves what is right and what is wrong, so they must rely on the government to make those decisions for them. But is he right?

---

[74] John Rawls, *A Theory of Justice,* (Cambridge, Mass.; Harvard University Press, 1971) 352.

The Bible says that each of us instinctively knows right from wrong because God has written it in our hearts.

> *For when Gentiles who do not have the Law do instinctively the things of the Law, these, not having the Law, are a law to themselves, 15) in that they show the work of the Law written in their hearts, their conscience bearing witness and their thoughts alternately accusing or else defending them.* **Romans 2:14-15**

This country was founded on preserving the principle of individual freedom which includes the right of individuals to make choices based on their conscience.

> "In the biblical sense, freedom does not mean the right to do whatever one pleases without any restraint whatever; rather, it means the liberty to make one's own decisions before God without restraint from government." [75]

Mr. Witmer did concede that the authority of one's conscience supersedes the authority of the state in matters of worship and evangelism, so why not in other areas? How can we please God if we act contrary to our knowledge of biblical truth and deny our conscience in matters of justice? Romans 14:22-23 is one place we find the concept of using our conscience to help us make wise decisions. It instructs Christians not to go against their conscience.

The Apostle Paul concludes that it was not wrong for Christians to eat meat sacrificed to idols, but if someone thought it was wrong and ate it anyway, it would be a sin indeed because he went against his own conscience.

---

[75] John Eidsmoe, *God and Caesar, Biblical Faith and Political Action,* Wipf and Stock Publishers, p. 84.

It is good not to eat meat or to drink wine, or to do anything by which your brother stumbles. 22) The faith which you have, have as your own conviction before God. Happy is he who does not condemn himself in what he approves [acts according to his conscience]. 23) But he who doubts is condemned if he eats [goes against his conscience], because his eating is not from faith; and whatever is not from faith is sin." **Romans 14:21-23**

So, if someone does something that is contrary to what he believes is right, he sins because he goes against his own conscience. Therefore, wouldn't it be wrong to obey a law that goes against conscience?

How could any Christian keep a clear conscience if, in the name of "Christian duty", he submits to a law or government action that causes harm to himself or his family? God never requires anyone to sacrifice his family, property or rights to appease an evil king or government.

To do righteousness and justice is desired by the Lord more than sacrifice. **Proverbs 21:3**

Norman L. Geisler did a good job of summing up the Christian's relationship with government as it relates to conscience. "...believers are always to obey government when it takes its place under God; they should never obey it when it takes the place of God... The authority of government ends where the conscience of the believer begins." [76]

Napoleon Bonaparte also recognized the importance of conscience:

---

[76] Norman L. Geisler, "A Premillennial View of Law and Government", *Bibliotheca Sacra Volume 142*, 567 (Dallas, TX: Dallas Theological Seminary, 1985), 262.

"Nobly did Napoleon Bonaparte, in the year 1804, recognize the rights of conscience in his reply to M. Martin, President of the Consistency of Geneva, in words worthy to be held in everlasting remembrance —'I wish it to be understood that my intention and my firm determination are to maintain liberty of worship. The empire of the law ends where the empire of the conscience begins. Neither the law nor the prince must infringe upon this empire.'" [77]

So what is a Christian to do when he cannot in good conscience obey a malicious or unjust mandate from the state? He will either do what is expedient and obey, or he will do what is right and disobey.

Therefore, to one who knows the right thing to do and does not do it, to him it is sin. **James 4:17**

The Scriptures do not give us clear or precise instructions as to when we should disobey an abusive authority, but they do give us many examples of people who disobeyed tyrants with God's blessing. This will be covered later in detail In Chapter 10, page 207 under the heading, *Examples of Biblical Civil Disobedience.*

Martin Luther, in his famed "Here I Stand" speech in 1521 before the emperor at the Diet of Worms, refused to go against his own conscience:

"Since then Your Majesty and your lordships desire a simple reply, I will answer without horns and without teeth. Unless I am convinced by Scripture and plain reason — I do not accept the authority of popes and councils, for they have contradicted each other —

---

[77] H. C. Fish, *Encyclopedia of 7700 Illustrations: Signs of the Times,* Paul Lee Tan, (Garland, TX: Bible Communications, Inc., 1996).

My conscience is captive to the Word of God. I cannot and I will not recant anything, for to go against conscience is neither right nor safe. God help me. Amen." [78]

Back to Mr. Witmer's assertion: "When the individual's conscience has authority over law, then government by law is jeopardized."

It appears that Mr. Witmer is concerned that anarchy would take over and reign supreme if individuals were free to act according to the dictates of their conscience. However, reason and common sense teach us:

A government that is jeopardized by people being true to their conscience is a government that needs to be changed or replaced.

Such a government is neither worthy of the people's allegiance nor does it deserve their submission.

If Mr. Witmer were correct, then the Declaration of Independence would be a shameful document that should be rejected. Remember? It declares that the people have the right and the duty to alter, abolish, or replace their government with one more to their liking. The reasons for breaking free from the tyranny of Great Britain did not pertain to worship only, but to justice and freedom as well.

In addition, it also declared that the colonists were dependent on the Law of Nature and Nature's God to guide them. It recognized God as the Creator and appealed to Him as the Supreme Judge of the World

---

[78] "Martin Luther to the Emperor at the Diet of Worms, Here I Stand Speech" *(1521)*. *Conservative Theological Journal, Volume 2.* 1998 (4) (54). Fort Worth, TX: Tyndale Theological Seminary.

to honor the righteousness of their intentions. It also relied on Divine Providence for support and protection.

The Bill of Rights like the Declaration of Independence was forged from the consciences of men who believed every individual has God-given rights that no one is allowed to ignore, not even the state. The Bill of Rights contains a partial list of our God-given rights that forbid any encroachment by the state of any kind, whatsoever.

> "That the Constitution of the United States established the basis for the rights of conscience was not an accident. The framers of that important document were well aware of the bloody history in the struggle for religious liberty experienced by many of their European ancestors. As I previously implied, religious liberty and the rights of conscience are like Siamese twins inseparably joined at the hip." [79]

Princeton theologian, Charles Hodge, holds a view that would place even more limitations on us: "We are to obey all that is in actual authority over us, whether their authority be legitimate or usurped, whether they are just or unjust." [80]

Some may agree with Mr. Hodge, but he has made a serious mistake in advocating unconditional obedience to authority. He has misunderstood a crucial issue we discussed earlier. It is not holding title of authority that makes authority legitimate or lawful. What makes it lawful is how it is administered. A tyrant's authority may be undeniable, but it is not legitimate when he uses

---

[79] Ron Merryman, *The Protection of Conscience: The Bible and Government (2009).*

[80] Charles Hodge, *Commentary on the Epistle to the Romans;* 1886 reprint, Grand Rapids: Wm. B. Eerdmans Publishing Co., 1947, p. 406.

it to oppress or abuse people. Would God remain just and righteous if He commanded us to voluntarily submit to the cruelty of a tyrant?

DUTY TO SUBMIT ENDS WHERE TYRANNY BEGINS

In Saudi Arabia, anyone who converts to Christianity can be beheaded by the state. Would a just God require clandestine Saudi Christians to obey the evil dictates of their malevolent leaders and turn Christian converts over to the state to be executed? Of course not.

Samuel Rutherford's view directly opposed Charles Hodge's and it harmonizes with the Scriptures:

> "Rutherford argued that Romans 13 indicates that all power is from God and that government is ordained and instituted by God. The state, however, is to be administered according to the principles of the Bible. Acts of the state that do not have a clear reference point in the Bible were considered to be illegitimate and acts of tyranny. Tyranny was defined as ruling without the sanction of God." [81]

Rutherford also held that:

> "A tyrannical government is always immoral. He considered it a work of Satan and... is not from God, and is not a power, but a licentious deviation of power, and is no more from God, but from sinful nature and the old serpent." [82]

---

[81] John H. Whitehead; *Christian Resistance In the Face of State Interference, Christianity and Civilization*, Geneva Divinity School, p. 10.

[82] *ibid*

The legitimacy, meaning the lawfulness, of a public servant is conditioned upon his or her promotion of freedom and justice.

> "The government's sole moral obligation is to preserve freedom. And freedom is the unfettered ability to choose to follow your own conscience and free will, not that of someone in the government. If the government keeps us safe but not free, the government will have become tyrannical and it will be as illegitimate [unlawful] as was the government of King George III in 1776. And it will be time for it to go." [83]

How can we be true to our conscience if we are required to obey every law, statute, code, and regulation no matter how illegitimate, unjust or immoral they are?

How can we, in good conscience, adopt the philosophy that we are essentially servants and the government is the master when it is contrary to our founding documents and the Bible?

> "Though man may establish rules or laws to be obeyed, if they are not reflections of the divine character of God, they are, to use Jesus' words, 'the traditions of men which pervert the law of God.' Such laws have set up the will of man against the will of God." [84]

---

[83] Judge Andrew P. Napolitano, *It Is Dangerous To Be Right When the Government Is Wrong*, p. 64.

[84] House, H. W. (1999). *Christian Ministries and the Law: Revised edition* (26).Grand Rapids, Mich. p. 156.

Did Jesus command his disciples to obey the traditions of men which pervert the law of God, Matt. 15:1-24? No, He would never do that. Then why would He require us to obey laws that pervert the Natural Law of God?

THE NATURAL LAW OF GOD

The Law of God is sometimes referred to as the Natural Law of God or Natural Law. When man's law is contrary to God's Natural Law, man's law is to be ignored.

> "**Natural laws**... [are] practical universal judgments which man himself elicits. These express necessary and obligatory rules of human conduct which have been established by the author of human nature as essential to the divine purpose in the universe and have been promulgated by God solely through human reason." [85]

James Otis was a lawyer and an author in colonial Massachusetts. He was a patriot who voiced his views against British policy that helped motivate the colonists to declare their independence. He is known for his catchphrase, 'Taxation without representation is tyranny.' He also said, 'The law of nature was not of man's making nor is it in his power to mend it or alter its course.'" [86]

Like James Otis, John Locke was an author who also addressed the issue of the Law of Nature.

---

[85] *Black's Law Dictionary*, Abridged Fifth Edition, West Publishing Co., 1983, p. 535.

[86] James Otis, *The Rights of British Colonies Asserted and Proved* (1764).

> "The Law of Nature stands as an Eternal Law of Men, Legislators as well as others. The Rules that they make for other men's Actions, must, as well as their own, and other Men's Actions, be conformable to the Law of Nature, i.e. to the Will of God." [87]

The colonists used every peaceful means available to them to be treated fairly, but when every effort failed, many of them simply refused to obey the unjust laws of the king because they were in violation of God's Natural Laws.

When the king sent his soldiers to take the arms and powder from the colonists at Lexington and Concord, he was violating God's Natural Law which gives every person the right of self-defense.

> "Christians are to be committed to Jesus Christ as Lord over all of life. This includes the way Christians respond to government. When the state demands worship or violation of the laws of God, it must be disobeyed (Acts 5:29). But when the state operates biblically in its proper sphere of authority, we must obey (Rom. 13:1-7)." [88]

Not all colonists thought it was right to resist the king's soldiers who were sent to enforce his laws and mandates. They accused their non-compliant neighbors of being traitors for their civil disobedience. It is true that civil disobedience sometimes turns into vigilantism by those who ignore the law and take matters into their own hands. However, that is not at all the same as refusing to obey a tyrant who uses extortion and coercion to subjugate people.

---

[87] John Locke, *Of Civil Government,* (1689).

[88] House, H. W. (1999). *Christian Ministries and The Law: Revised edition (26)*. Grand Rapids, Mich.) p. 152.

> "The breaking of an unjust law, as civil disobedience is at times defined, need not necessarily reflect a spirit of anarchy, criminal intent, or general contempt for laws. It may in fact, reflect an earnest desire to respect the Rule of Law and to test the validity of a specific law and so to provide a larger measure of justice." [89]

Richard Bardolph also addressed this issue:

> "Disobedience to immoral law is not disrespectful of law in general. Civil disobedience 'in its purest form'... breaks laws that law may prevail. Failure to comply with specific civil demands is not equivalent to general rebellion." [90]

There are many clear examples of civil disobedience in the Bible where God blessed, rather than punished, those who refused to submit to tyranny. See Chapter 9, OPTIONS FOR KEEPING FREEDOM, pg. 185.

It appears that most Christians today are either ignorant or unwilling to recognize the true limits placed on government and are either afraid or reluctant to stand up to crooked politicians when they cross over the line.

They are afraid of what the government might do to them if they, for example, stop paying unconstitutional confiscatory taxes, carry a gun without a license, refuse to wear a seatbelt, or spank their misbehaving children. So they remain silent while the government ignores their

---

[89] *The Commission on Theology and Church Relations of the Lutheran Church,* Missouri Synod, 379. ("Civil Obedience & Disobedience").

[90] Richard Bardolph, "Some Reflections on Civil Disobedience", *Concordia Theological Monthly 38*, no. 6 (June 1967), 381.

rights, spies on them, ruins their healthcare, and burdens future generations with crushing government debt.

Some even believe that voicing displeasure against such abuses would be unpatriotic or unbiblical. So they need to pay close attention to what John H. Whitehead has to say:

> "It is not foreign to Christianity to protest the illegitimate acts of civil government. The Christian must then say both yes and no to the state. Total silence by the church is received by the state as an endorsement of all that it does, but it is viewed as an act of treason by God. In fact, the Bible proclaims: *A righteous man falling down before the wicked is a troubled fountain, and a corrupt spring, **Prov. 25:26**.*" [90a]

[90a] John H. Whitehead; 'Christian Resistance In the Face of State Interference", *Christianity and Civilization,* Geneva Divinity School, p. 9.

CHAPTER 6

VIEWPOINT 3

Limited Authority in Matters of Faith and Freedom

Those who hold to this viewpoint, including yours truly, believe that God limits the authority of government not only in matters of faith, but also in matters of freedom.

Even before the Declaration of Independence was written, colonists held this viewpoint. They wrote a strongly worded Declaration of Rights that recognized the limited authority of government in matters concerning faith and freedom.

> "That the inhabitants of the English Colonies in North America, by immutable laws of nature, the principles of the English Constitution, and the several charters or compacts, have the following rights: RESOLVED, N.C.D. 1. That they are entitled to life, liberty, and property, and they never ceded to any sovereign power whatever, a right to dispose of either without their consent." [91]

Our founding fathers fought a long bloody war because they would not compromise their beliefs. Some of them were:

- God has given all mankind unalienable rights, including life, liberty, and property.

---

[91] "Declaration of Rights", October 14, 1774, *Journals of the Continental Congress, 1774-1789.*

- The purpose of government is to respect and protect the rights of the people.
- When government abuses those rights, it loses its right to govern.
- **"Resistance to tyranny is obedience to God."** This became the motto of the Colonists.

The Colonists grew in their resolve and confidence in God to the point where one Crown-appointed governor wrote about their attitude to the Board of Trade back in England: "If you ask an American, who is his master, he will tell you he has none, nor any governor but Jesus Christ." [92]

The Committees of Correspondence picked up the following phrase and began sounding the cry across the Colonies: "No King but King Jesus!" [93]

We study our founding fathers because they faced many of the same issues and decisions we do. If they were wrong to resist the tyranny over them, then we would be wrong to resist the tyranny over us. The Declaration of Independence is arguably our most precious national treasure. However, if resisting an authority that is abusive is wrong and contrary to the Scriptures, then The Declaration of Independence should be repudiated and condemned along with our founding fathers who gave their lives for the principles it declares.

---

[92] Hezekiah Niles, *Principles and Acts of the Revolution in America* (Baltimore: William Ogden Niles, 1822), p. 418.

[93] Peter Powers, Election Sermon entitled "Jesus Christ the King" (Newburyport, 1778). Clifford K. Shipton, *Sibley's Harvard Graduates* (Boston: Massachusetts Historical Society, 1965), Vol. XIII, pp. 475-476.

Isn't it contradictory and hypocritical for people to say that it's wrong to resist government when it attacks our freedoms but then praise and celebrate our forefathers who did that very thing?

If the colonists were wrong to resist tyranny and the Declaration of Independence is contrary to God's established order, then the 4th of July should cease to be a national holiday and our founding fathers should be considered traitors.

DECLARATION OF INDEPENDENCE CITATIONS

Let's take a look at some of the more well-known parts of the Declaration of Independence to see if they are in accord with God's Word.

> "We hold these truths to be self-evident, that all men are created equal, that they are endowed by their Creator with certain unalienable Rights that among these are Life, Liberty, and the pursuit of Happiness."

These are beautiful words because they are true and they bring glory to God. They are words that turned the world system upside down along with its enslaving philosophy of the divine right of kings.

God gives stern warnings to rulers who violate the sacred rights He gave to us. Governing authorities all over the world need to read and heed the following verses:

> *Woe to those who enact evil statutes, and to those who constantly record unjust decisions, 2) so as to deprive the needy of justice, and rob the poor of My people of their rights, in order that widows may be their spoil, and that they may plunder the orphans.*
> **_Isaiah 10:1-2_**

Woe to those who are wise in their own eyes, and clever in their own sight! 23) Who justify the wicked for a bribe, and take away the rights of the ones who are in the right! **Isaiah 5:21&23**

The righteous is concerned for the rights of the poor. The wicked does not understand such concern. **Proverbs 29:7**

Open your mouth for the mute, for the rights of all the unfortunate. 9) Open your mouth, judge righteously, and defend the rights of the afflicted and needy. **Proverbs 31:8-9**

OUR RIGHTS COME FROM GOD

Every person has been given immutable rights from God including the poor, afflicted, and needy.

> "The basis for any claim that Christians have the right to civil disobedience rests on the fact that government has only limited authority, and that men have certain God-given rights that government cannot violate." [94]

The historian, George Bancroft, expressed the following view in his oration in 1826 on the fiftieth anniversary of the signing of the Declaration of Independence. 'I welcome you to a profession of the principles of public justice which emanate directly from God! These principles are eternal not only in their truth but in their efficacy [effectiveness].'"

---

[94] John Eidsmoe, *God and Caesar, Biblical Faith and Political Action,* Wipf and Stock Publishers, p. 90, Barton, D. (2003). *Celebrate Liberty! Famous Patriotic Speeches & Sermons (84-85).* Aledo, TX: Wall Builders Press.

Principles of justice are based on natural law and the rights that God has bestowed to all mankind. "God alone is the inciter and guarantor of freedom. Political freedom, as the Western world has known it, is only a political reading of the Bible. Religion and freedom are indivisible." [95]

For those who deny the idea that our individual rights come from God, the question is: "Then, from where do they come?" At the time the Declaration was written, many thought their rights came from the king. Likewise today, many think their rights come from the President, Congress, or the Supreme Court. It is clear that such thinking is at odds with the brave signers and supporters of that great declaration. They believed that our rights come from God, not from a king or from any other human ruler.

> *It was for freedom that Christ set us free; therefore keep standing firm and do not be subject again to a yoke of slavery.* **Galatians 5:1**

> *Now the Lord is the Spirit; and where the Spirit of the Lord is, there is liberty.* **2 Corinthians 3:17**

Christ has not only set us free from the curse of sin, condemnation and legalism, but He also gave us free will to follow our conscience without interference or coercion from government.

GOVERNMENT IS TO PROTECT & SECURE OUR RIGHTS

The Declaration continues:

> "...that to secure these rights, governments are instituted by Men...."

---

[95] Whittaker Chambers, *Witness,* (New York Random House, 1952) p. 16.

Is the purpose of government to secure the God-given rights of the people? Absolutely. God did not ordain government to force people to submit to the wicked whims of power-mad autocrats.

Government protects and secures the rights of the people, punishes those who do evil and praises those who do what is right. That includes protecting people from any threat of evil whether it be foreign or domestic and whether it is within or without the government.

> "That the sole object and only legitimate end of government is to protect the citizen in the enjoyment of life, liberty, and property, and when the government assumes other functions it is usurpation and oppression." [96]

Government is a divine institution ordained by God that is administered by man. When the "higher-powers" who are the ministers of government submit to God, the "Highest Power", then the rights of the people are secure and there is blessing in the land.

The Declaration rightly placed the responsibility to protect the rights and freedoms of the people on the government but never made it responsible to provide for their every want and need.

The Declaration continues:

> "...deriving their just power from the consent of the governed."

God did not create man for government. He created government for man. Both are under Him and both are responsible to Him. When government acts as a minister

---

[96] *Alabama, Declaration of Rights Article I Section 35.*

of God for good, man is required by God to submit. When government acts as a minister of Satan for evil, man is not required by God to submit. In that sense, government derives its just power from the consent of the governed.

THE RIGHT TO ALTER OR ABOLISH GOVERNMENT

The Declaration continues:

> "That whenever any form of government becomes destructive to these ends [protecting the rights of the people], it is the Right of the People to alter or to abolish it, and to institute new government...."

It is unfortunate that the majority of Americans don't know that they have the right to alter, abolish, separate from any government that ignores their rights, and to form a new one. Those who question whether this right is biblical should consider the following:

When King Solomon died, his son, Rehoboam, took over his father's throne. He told the people he would discipline them with whips and scorpions, 1 Kings 12:11. That caused the nation of Israel to split into two parts. Ten tribes separated from Rehoboam and went north to form the Northern Kingdom under their new king, Jeroboam. The two tribes remaining under Rehoboam's reign became known as the Southern Kingdom.

Did God condemn Jeroboam or the people of the Northern Kingdom for refusing to submit and for separating from Rehoboam to form a new kingdom? Here's what God said to Jeroboam, the new king:

> *I will take the kingdom from his son's hand* [Rehoboam, the son of Solomon] *and give it to you* [Jeroboam], *even ten tribes.* **1 Kings 11:35**
>
> *I will take you* [Jeroboam], *and you shall reign over whatever you desire, and you shall be king over Israel* [the Northern Kingdom was called Israel]. *38) Then it will be, that if you listen to all that I command you and walk in My ways, and do what is right in My sight by observing My statutes and My commandments, as My servant David did, then I will be with you and build you an enduring house as I built for David, and I will give Israel to you.* **1 Kings 11:37-38**

God made this promise to Jeroboam after he led the people away from Rehoboam who forfeited his right to rule when he refused to recognize the rights of his people and even threatened to oppress them. The Israelites were correct in refusing to submit to his tyranny and in following Jeroboam. They seceded from the union of twelve tribes to form a new nation.

Did God punish them? No, on the contrary, He promised great blessings to Jeroboam if he would rule the new kingdom in obedience to Him.

CHAPTER 7

ROMANS 13

The first seven verses of Romans 13 cover the relationship between Christians and government in more detail than any other Scriptures. They are shown below as they appear in the New American Standard Version of the Bible.

ROMANS 13:1-7

1) Let every person be in subjection to the governing authorities. For there is no authority except from God, and those which exist are established by God.

2) Therefore he who resists authority has opposed the ordinance of God; and they who have opposed will receive condemnation upon themselves.

3) For rulers are not a cause of fear for good behavior, but for evil. Do you want to have no fear of authority? Do what is good, and you will have praise from the same;

4) For it is a minister of God to you for good. But if you do what is evil, be afraid; for it does not bear the sword for nothing; for it is a minister of God, an avenger who brings wrath upon the one who practices evil.

5) Wherefore it is necessary to be in subjection, not only because of wrath, but also for conscience sake.

6) For because of this you also pay taxes, for rulers are servants of God, devoting themselves to this very thing.

7) *Render to all what is due them: tax to whom tax is due; custom to whom custom; fear to whom fear; honor to whom honor.*

MISUNDERSTOOD & MISAPPLIED

It is amazing how one person can read these seven verses and get one meaning while someone else can read them and get a totally different one. But the Scriptures have only one correct meaning, so they must be studied closely, considering all other pertinent Scriptures and taking into account the historical context and grammar of the original languages in order to insure accuracy.

Since most people don't have the time or the ability to do that, they rely on pastors who have been trained to exegete Scriptures line upon line and precept upon precept from the original languages. They usually can be trusted to rightly divide the Word of truth.

> *Study to show yourself approved unto God, a workman that needs not to be ashamed, rightly dividing the word of truth.* **2 Timothy 2:15**

The view that Romans 13:1-7 or 2 Peter 1:13-15 were written to compel believers to submit to tyranny is biblically incorrect. Consider the following three points:

1. None of the verses in question state that we must submit unconditionally to civil government even though some people impose that idea on the text. In fact, there are no Scriptures in the entire Bible that teach that.

2. Proper hermeneutics forbids such a conclusion. There are many examples in the Bible of people who disobeyed civil government and were blessed

> by God for doing so as we'll see in Chapter 10, "Examples of Biblical Civil Disobedience".

> 3. There are clauses in the Romans 13 and 1 Peter passages that limit civil government. Only rulers who function as "ministers of God for good" have authorization from God, Rom. 13:4. Good citizens have nothing to fear from God's ministers; in fact, they may receive praise from them for their good behavior, Rom. 13: 3 and 1 Pet. 2:14. This certainly does not apply to rulers who abuse people they have pledged to serve.

Still, many believe that Romans 13:1-7 requires unconditional submission and so they feel obligated to stand idly by while their government enslaves them.

> "Romans chapter 13 has become a kind of ubiquitous opiate that causes Christians to revel in sheepish slavery and servitude... [and has] caused more Christians to surrender their God-given liberties and freedoms to all sorts of tyrants, both secular and religious." [97]

One of the main reasons people misunderstand these seven verses is because they fail to recognize that they do not refer to *all* governing rulers. They refer only to those who submit to God's authority and function as His ministers for good. All other rulers are under His condemnation, not His blessing.

These verses define the ideal government from God's divine perspective as one that operates properly as His minister for good, possessing legitimate authority to punish evildoers.

---

[97] Timothy Baldwin and Chuck Baldwin, *Romans 13, The True Meaning of Submission,* p. 11.

To apply the submission that <u>Romans 13:1-7</u> requires to a tyrannical government that has become a minister of Satan for evil is a gross misapplication!

> "Nothing in the entire passage has any reference to wicked rulers. It says not one word about rebellious magistrates; or those who oppose God; or those who become despotic and tyrannical in their abuse of power. None of these sorts of governments are addressed or described here at all. Rather, the whole point of the passage is simply to clarify that there is indeed a God-ordained purpose for civil government." [98]

On January 30, 1750, Jonathan Mayhew delivered a sermon on <u>Romans 13:1-7</u>.

> "The apostle's [Paul] doctrine… may be summed up in the following observations, viz.: That the end of magistracy is the good of civil society… That civil rulers, as such, are the ordinance and ministers of God; it being by His permission and providence that any bear rule and agreeable to His will that there should be some persons vested with authority in society, for the well-being of it… It is obvious then, in general, that the civil rulers whom the apostle speaks of, and obedience to whom he presses upon Christians as a duty, are good rulers, such as are, in the exercise of their office and power, benefactors to society.…" [99]

---

[98] Runyan, Gordan (2012-08-24). *Resistance to Tyrants: Romans 13 and the Christian Duty to Oppose Wicked Rulers* (p. 38). Happy Siege. Kindle Edition.

[99] Mayhew, Jonathan, "Discourse Concerning Unlimited Submission and Non-resistance to the Higher Powers, etc., etc." January 30, 1750, in the sermon, "The Annals of America", 20 vols. (Chicago, IL: *Encyclopedia Britannica*, 1968), Vol. 1, pp. 482-483.

In the earlier chapters of Romans, Paul stressed the Good News of salvation through faith in Christ and how it set us free from servitude to the Mosaic Law. But there was the possibility that believers of his day might misunderstand this newly acquired freedom and misuse it to support a growing anti-government viewpoint that had developed out of hatred for the Roman conquerors who had taken over their land.

Runyan Gordan describes their erroneous viewpoint in what could have been their own words:

> "I used to be under the [Mosaic] law. Now, Christ has set me free. Not under law but under grace. If I am no longer bound under the jurisdiction of the Law of God in this manner, then surely no merely human laws or governments can have any authority over me! If I'm free from servile life under God's own Law, how much less could any government of man command my service?" [100]

Romans 13:1-7 very clearly condemns lawlessness and anarchy which is the mindset described above. So Paul corrected this problem, not by requiring unconditional submission to an abusive government but by describing a government that operates as a minister of God for good where submission is required.

ROMANS 13:1   SUBMISSION TO GOD'S DELEGATED AUTHORITIES

Let every person be in subjection to the governing authorities. For there is no authority except from God, and those which exist are established by God.

---

[100] Runyan, Gordan (2012-08-24). *Resistance to Tyrants: Romans 13 and the Christian Duty to Oppose Wicked Rulers* (p. 8). Happy Siege. Kindle Edition.

This verse gives a very general statement concerning God's establishment of government and the universal concept of authority and submission. Set apart by itself, it gives rise to several questions. Is it demanding unconditional submission to all governments, including those that are despotic?

> "Perhaps the best solution, then, is to view [Romans] 13:1-7 as a general statement about how the Christian should relate to government, with exceptions to this advice assumed but not spelled out here." [101]

Since this verse leaves a lot of "What if...?" questions unanswered, let's break it down piece by piece:

Romans 13:1 (a)

Let every person be in subjection to the governing authorities...

We know that people holding to Viewpoint One believe this sentence is all that needs to be said because it requires everyone to submit to governing authorities, even if they are tyrants.

However, Everett Harrison sheds light on the issue by pointing out that tyrants are not the subject of this passage. They are not under consideration or relevant in these verses.

> "'The presentation [Romans 13:1-7] seems to take no account of the possibility that government may be

---

[101] D. A. Carson, *New Bible Commentary :*21st Century Edition, Rev. Ed. of: *The New Bible Commentary.*3rd Ed. /Edited by D. Guthrie, J.A. Motyer. 1970., 4th ed. (Leicester, England; Downers Grove, Ill., USA: Inter-Varsity Press, 1994), Ro 12:9.

tyrannical and may reward evil and suppress good', notes Everett Harrison. Why? Paul's silence probably means he is dealing with the 'norm', with the state that fulfills the ideal for government. But recognize one thing: Paul does not call for absolute obedience to everything the state demands, or for a willingness to comply at any cost for the sake of security. He deals instead with the mandate God gives to government and with the way a government should function." [102]

"Governing authorities" are supposed to enforce God's laws and God's will, not their own. Every person, no matter what his or her position in life may be, must answer to authority. A more literal rendering of "governing authorities" from the Greek is **"higher powers"**. Everyone has a "higher power" over him to whom he is required to submit, and that includes those in government.

Ideally: Children submit to parents. Wives submit to husbands. Employees submit to their bosses. CEOs submit to the board of directors. The board of directors submits to the shareholders. People submit to police officers. Police officers submit to judges and judges submit to Congress. Congress and the President submit to the Constitution, and everyone inevitably answers to the ultimate authority which is God.

"Romans 13:1-7 describes a general principle to all human beings for all times of what higher powers are, how they are ordained of God, and under what

---

[102] E.F. Harrison, "Romans", *The Expositor's Bible Commentary*, vol. 10, ed. F.E. Gabelein (Grand Rapids: Zondervan, 1976) p. 137; *The Duty of Civil Disobedience to the Government: Contemporary Struggles Between Christians and the State,* H. Wayne House, p. 147.

conditions are they made the ministers of God, and when they are thus to be submitted to." [103]

Romans 13:1 (b)

... for there is no [legitimate] *authority except from God, and those which exist are established by God.*

J. B. PHILLIPS N. T. TRANSLATION:
Every Christian ought to obey the civil authorities, for all legitimate authority is derived from God's authority...

It should be understood that all legitimate or lawful authority comes from God, so no one can ascribe absolute authority to himself. When one assumes authority that is not from God, then it is counterfeit, illegitimate, unlawful, and therefore requires neither respect nor submission.

Dictators, tyrants, despots, warlords, mafia heads, leaders of street gangs, etc. certainly have authority that they assert, but it is illegitimate because it has not been delegated to them from God. They do not submit to Him or His laws, but instead, act contrary to His Just and Righteous standards.

> "Paul states very clearly in Romans 13:1 that all government is ordained and established by God. In the Bible, parents, pastors, civil authorities, employers, and others are said to have received their authority to govern from God. This authority, however, is delegated authority. It is not to be exercised independent of God's Word. In fact, the Bible recognizes no power independent of God. (Romans 13:1) For any delegated sphere of authority

---

[103] Chuck and Timothy Baldwin, *Romans 13, The True Meaning of Submission*, 2011, p. 20.

to speak of itself as a power independent from God is rebellion against Him. For the courts, the Internal Revenue Service, and other civil agencies to speak of their authority as being over all areas of life and as being derived from the state, is blasphemy." [104]

A man may become king or be elected president, but if he is an autocrat, he has no appointment from God. God rebuked Israel when He said:

They have set up kings, but not by Me.... **Hosea 8:4**

People must be able to determine when authority is legitimate and when it is not, which laws are valid and which ones are not. When people cannot distinguish between these, tyrants cannot be deterred.

"He [the believer] has therefore the freedom, the free will, the self-determination to choose between legitimate and illegitimate authority; legitimate authority delegated by God; illegitimate authority provided through the satanic administration of the ruler-ship of this world. Therefore, all human authority is a matter of human choice, human volition. Legitimate authority won't work unless someone accepts that authority, and even illegitimate authority won't work unless someone accepts that authority." [105]

Any law, code, rule, regulation or statute that goes beyond the Constitution or is contrary to it, is counterfeit, illegitimate, unlawful, and therefore requires no respect or submission.

---

[104] John H. Whitehead; *Christianity and Civilization: The Theology of Christian Resistance,* "Christian Resistance in the Face of State Interference", Geneva Divinity School Press, 1983, p. 5.

[105] R.B. Theime Jr., *Unpublished Class Notes,* "Revelation 2".

"All laws which are repugnant to the Constitution are null and void." [106]

"An unconstitutional act is not law; it confers no rights, imposes no duties; affords no protection; it creates no office; it is in legal contemplation as inoperative as though it had never been passed." [107]

The media and politicians have convinced most people that our government is all-powerful and can fix any problem simply by creating new laws. The trouble is, most of these laws ignore the Constitution and the natural laws of God.

"It's [the Constitution's] conception of power was Christian: power is ministerial, not legislative, i.e., powers in any area, church, state, school, or family, are not endowed with ability to create laws apart from the higher law but only to administer fundamental law as man is able to grasp and approximate it. *Civil government is thus an administrator rather than a creator of law; it is not sovereign over law but is under law.* The doctrine of express powers [government has only the powers expressed in the Constitution] is a strong limitation on even the administrative or ministerial role of civil government." [108]

Thank God our founding fathers designed our country to operate under the **Rule of Law** established by the Constitution rather than operate under the caprice of men.

"We in the United States of America do not live under

---

[106] *Marbury vs. Maddison,* 5 US (2 Cranch) 137, 174, 176, (1803) [emphasis added].

[107] Norton vs. Shelby County, 118 US 425 p. 442.

[108] Rousas Hohn Rushdoony, *This Independent Republic,* 2001 pp.35-36 [emphasis added].

> a monarchy. We have no king. There is no single governing official in this country. America's 'supreme Law' does not rest with any man or any group of men. America's 'supreme Law' does not rest with the President, the Congress, or even the Supreme Court. In America, the U.S. Constitution is the 'supreme Law of the Land'. Under our laws, every governing official publicly promises to submit to the Constitution of the United States. Do readers understand the significance of this distinction? I hope so ... This means that in America the 'higher powers' are not the men who occupy elected office; they are the tenets and principles set forth in the U.S. Constitution. Under our laws and form of government, it is the duty of every citizen, including our elected officials, to obey the U.S. Constitution." [109]

The United States has wonderful, natural resources and hard-working people, but what separates us from all other countries is that we recognize that our rights come from God and our government is subordinate to the Constitution.

> "The people themselves are the government in our system, and the true law of the land is not found in the courts or in the legislatures but in the Constitution of the federal government and in the Constitutions of the several States." [110]

Because God's law exceeds the authority of man's laws, any law, statute, code, or rule that is contrary to God's Law requires no submission.

---

[109] *http://chuckbaldwinlive.com/Articles/tabid/109/ID/511/Romans-Chapter-13.aspx*

[110] H. Wayne House, *The Duty of Civil Disobedience to the Government: Contemporary Struggles Between Christians and the State*, p. 170.

"Human laws are only valid and good in so far as they conform to His [God's] law, explaining and applying it; they are bad whenever they contradict or disregard it; and it is then not only your right, but your duty, to disobey them and abolish them... You have not, and cannot have, any master but God, without being false and rebellious to Him." [111]

William Blackstone, the great legal mind of the 18th century, certainly understood that the Bible trumps the State whenever they are at odds.

"Blackstone, like Montesquieu, also derived his political and legal philosophy from the Bible. The premise behind Blackstone's commentaries is that the Creator has revealed fixed principles in nature and Scripture. Therefore, the function of human law is to cooperate or operate in harmony with these fixed principles rather than operate in rebellion against them." [112]

"Thus, when the Supreme Being formed the universe, and created matter out of nothing, He imposed certain principles upon that matter, from which it can never depart, and without which it would cease to be... If we farther advance, from mere inactive matter to vegetable and animal life, we shall find them governed by laws, more numerous indeed but equally fixed and invariable... Man, considered as a creature, must necessarily be subject to the laws of his Creator, for he is entirely a dependent being... *no human laws should be suffered to contradict the laws of nature and the law of revelation.*" [Emphasis added] [113]

---

[111] Giuseppe Mazzini, *The Duties of Man,* (1805-1872) p. 32.

[112] Dr. Andy Woods, *Darwin, Evolution, and the American Constitution,* March 2011, p. 81.

[113] Sir William Blackstone, *Commentaries on the Laws of New England,* 5 volumes, 1771, 1:38-39, 42.

The Bill of Rights also puts limits on those who rule and makes them responsible to God and to the people to stay within those limits.

> "God desires that every man should have the unimpaired and divine right of choice as long as that choice does not violate the right of our neighbor to make his own choices." [114]

God has never given anyone the authority to take away our freedom to live according to our convictions, and that especially applies to tyrants who try to force us to submit to their dictates against our will.

There must be a balance between the freedom of the people and the authority of the government.

> "Freedom without authority becomes anarchy, in which no one is free; but authority without freedom is tyranny, which ceases to be legitimate authority. No tyrant can remain in power without the consent and cooperation of his victims." [115]

Wow, what a statement! It's worth reading again.

Consent and cooperation enables tyrants.

God used dictators and tyrants from pagan countries to discipline the Israelites for their disobedience, but that does not mean that cruelty is sanctioned by God. It isn't. But He can and does use illegitimate authority-wielding tyrants to achieve His purpose. Using an evil, pagan nation to discipline Israel does not mean God

---

[114] Gregory Williams, "Romans 13 & Christ's Clergy Response Teams", *NewsWithViews.com*, 1-21-09.

[115] R.B. Theime Jr., *Christian Integrity,* p. 72.

has sanctioned it as a lawful authority. Here is the point:

Anyone who uses his authority to abuse others did not receive it from God. God never condones abusive authority.

> *They* [the Chaldeans] *are dreaded and feared. Their justice and authority originate with themselves.* **Habakkuk 1:7**

The Chaldeans who were also known as Babylonians were cruel pagans whose ruthless king, named "Nebuchadnezzar", believed he was answerable to no one, not even to God.

Yet God used Nebuchadnezzar to discipline His people even though He did not approve of him or bless him. Quite the opposite... God demonstrated His omnipotence to King Nebuchadnezzar by striking him down with a horrible disease. That brought him to a state of humility and he eventually became a believer, Dan. 4:30-37.

It is difficult for some people to accept the fact that our nation has essentially abandoned the **Rule of Law** under the Constitution and now operates unconstitutionally through executive orders, statutes, codes, rules, and regulations that have not been enacted into positive law. **Positive law** is a law where its exact words have been approved and passed by Congress.

The federal government has grown so large and so corrupt that it makes little difference which political party controls any branch of it. Extremely rich power-brokers have the ability and means to buy nearly any politician they desire; they can outspend all the political parties and individual contributors combined. Any candidate that goes against the establishment, i.e. insiders in Washington D.C., will subsequently be attacked by the media because it is also owned and financed by power-brokers who prefer to remain anonymous.

The Federal Reserve, a private corporation, illustrates the point. It is owned and controlled by international bankers who operate in such secrecy that their names remain unknown. And we have allowed this powerful, unelected, foreign group of people to control the entire economy of the U.S.

ROMANS 13:2   PUNISHMENT FOR RESISTING LEGITIMATE AUTHORITY

(a) Therefore he who <u>resists</u> authority has opposed the <u>ordinance</u> of God; (b) and they who have opposed will receive condemnation upon themselves.

The first few words appear in other versions of the Bible as follows:

"Whosoever therefore resists... " (KJV & NKJV)
"Therefore whoever resists... " (ESV)
The context includes anyone and everyone, whether citizen or ruler.

"Resists" is used metaphorically to set oneself in opposition or in array against something or someone; to resist. The one who resists the order of authority established by God is actually opposing God.

"Ordinance" comes from the Greek word "diatage" meaning order or arrangement. Here it refers to the order or arrangement of authority from God.

> "The man who withstands the official authority ordained by God is in conflict with God's "ordinance" according to Romans 13:2. Obviously this does not mean that every governmental decree is God's ordinance. διαταγή [diatage] refers rather to God's 'ordaining' according to verse 1b." [116]

Romans 13:2 is based on the premise of verse 1b concerning legitimate authority being established by God. Anyone who resists legitimate authority is opposing the ordinance of God whether he is a citizen who robs a bank or a government official who subjugates the people.

Many have misunderstood this verse because they think it pertains only to the people but not to their leaders. However, it applies to both because both answer to God for their actions. In our system of government, office-holders are not only answerable to God, they are supposed to answer to the people as well.

> "Magistrates may hence learn what their vocation is, for they are not to rule for their own interest, but for the public good, nor are they endued with unbridled power, but what is restricted to the wellbeing of their subjects; in short, they are responsible to God and to men in the exercise of their power." [117]

All authority that is delegated by God is limited and is legitimate. The moment a husband, parent, pastor, boss, policeman, judge, senator, congressman, or president abuses those under his or her authority, their

---

[116] *Theological Dictionary of the New Testament.*

[117] John Calvin, *Commentaries on the Epistle of Paul the Apostle to the Romans*, (1539) John Owen translation (1849) p. 481.

authority becomes illegitimate and is in opposition to God. They have crossed the line from being a servant of God to being a rebel against Him.

When governing officials raise their right hands to make a solemn oath to abide by the Constitution saying, "...so help me God", and then defiantly break that oath by violating our rights over and over again, they dishonor themselves and forfeit their right to govern. Here is another look at the first part of verse 2:

Romans 13:2 (a)

Therefore he [citizen or ruler] ***who resists*** [legitimate/lawful] ***authority has opposed the ordinance*** [the order or arrangement of authority] ***of God....***

> "It should be noted that [John] Adams, in opposing the idea of sovereignty, insisted on the necessity of a double responsibility in civil government, to 'earth' i.e., society, and to 'heaven' or God. Responsibility connotes subordination; we are under those to whom we are responsible... Man, however, and civil government are and must be responsible agencies. If transcendental responsibility, the subordination to God [by government], be removed, then man becomes a creature of the state and responsible to it, and the aseity or self-derived being of the state is asserted." [118]

It is important to recognize that Romans 13, verses 1 & 2 emphasize God's arrangement of authority. Rulers are under God's authority and citizens are under the rulers' authority. When both submit to the authority

---

[118] Rousas John Rushdoony, *This Independent Republic*, Ross House Books, 1964, p. 36.

over them, all is well. When either one fails to submit to God's arrangement of authority, they receive God's condemnation.

Romans 13:2 (b)

...and they [citizens or rulers] ***who have opposed*** [God's arrangement of authority] ***will receive condemnation upon themselves.***

People who are unaware that both citizen *and ruler* must subordinate themselves to the authority of God and the Constitution tend to cower when intimidated or threatened by government bullies. However, if they were aware that rulers must be subordinate to their higher authority as well, they might be more prone to stand up to these tormentors and insist that their rights be respected.

ROMANS 13:3   LEGITIMATE RULERS RESPECT GOOD BEHAVIOR

(a) For rulers are not a cause of fear for good behavior, but for evil. Do you want to have no fear of authority? (b) Do what is good, and you will have praise from the same.

This verse continues to express the viewpoint of rulers functioning under the authority structure designed by God. This means that they are not opposing God but are submitting to Him and acting as His servants.

We would describe them as legitimate rulers who stay within the confines of their constitutional limitations and recognize the God-given rights of individual citizens. In no way is this verse referring to evil rulers who are perpetuating corruption in governments.

> "We know that many thousands of Christians in Rome were executed for proclaiming faith in Christ! It is astounding that some would have us believe Paul was describing this government when he spoke of God's servant, who is no threat to good works... To insert a wicked government into this Bible text not only overturns the text itself, but would end up committing spiritual treason, by giving aid and comfort to the enemies of God and His Christ." [119]

Romans 13:3 (a)

For rulers are not a cause of fear for good behavior, but for evil...

People with good behavior don't normally commit crimes, so they should have nothing to fear from their rulers. But criminals have good reason to fear rulers because God has given them the authority to punish evildoers. This is good and proper. However, it is neither good nor proper when well-behaved, law-abiding people fear their government.

> "When the people fear the government, there is tyranny; when the government fears the people, there is liberty."
> ~ Thomas Jefferson ~

People should obey laws because they are constitutional, just and in accord with God's natural law, not because they fear their government. Most people know little if anything about God's natural law and are unaware of its importance. However, God's natural law is the ultimate law which is over every person in every place.

---

[119] Runyan, Gordan (2012-08-24). *Resistance to Tyrants: Romans 13 and the Christian Duty to Oppose Wicked Rulers* (p. 31). Happy Siege. Kindle Edition.

The signers of the Declaration of Independence understood this when they risked their lives to adhere to it rather than the arbitrary, freedom-destroying laws of their king. It is mentioned in the first sentence of the Declaration.

> "When in the course of human events, it becomes necessary for one people to dissolve the political bands which have connected them with another, and to assume among the powers of the earth, the separate and equal station to which the <u>Laws of Nature and of Nature's God</u> entitles them...." [120]

WHAT IS GOOD BEHAVIOR?

The Bible covers this in the following verses:

> *Therefore, however you want people to treat you, so treat them, for this is the Law and the Prophets.* **Matthew 7:12**

> *And just as you want people to treat you, treat them in the same way.* **Luke 6:31**

> "Along with the Ten Commandments, the Bible's most famous document, no piece of legislation ever enacted has influenced human behavior as much as the biblical injunction to 'Love your neighbor as yourself' (Leviticus 19:18)... [It] establishes the imperative of treating people with justice and compassion, and introduced the Golden Rule to the world; the Exodus narrative made clear that, despite the inequities of this world, God intends that ultimately people be free." [121]

---

[120] "Declaration of Independence", (1st part of 1st paragraph).

[121] Rabbi Joseph Telushkin, *Biblical Literacy: The Most Important People, Events, and Ideas of the Hebrew Bible* (1997) p. xxi.

Richard J. Maybury wrote the series of books called *Uncle Eric's Model of How the World Works*. Below is a sample of his sage advice from one of his books that gives two basic laws defining good behavior.

> "Some people will wait for disaster to swallow them up, and others will choose like America's founders to passionately fight for a nation, conceived in liberty and dedicated to the two fundamental laws that make an advanced civilization possible. The Two Laws:
>
> 1) Do all you have agreed to do.
> 2) Do not encroach on other persons or their property." [122]

Just think how wonderful it would be if the myriad of regulations were abolished and a person had the right to do anything he pleased as long as he didn't infringe on the rights of others. THAT is true freedom!

If you want to carry a gun for protection, no problem. You're not infringing on the rights of others. If you want to drive without a seatbelt, no problem. You're not infringing on the rights of others. If you want to get married and want to record it in the family Bible rather than paying for a license from the STATE, no problem.

You're not infringing on the rights of others. If you want to (fill in the blank) _____, just make sure you're not infringing on the rights of others. You get the idea.

---

[122] Richard J. Maybury, *Ancient Rome, How It Affects You Today,* 2004, Bluestocking Press, p. 94-95.

God has given rulers the authority to punish evildoers and *only* evildoers. Those who do not encroach on the rights of others should be praised, not punished. And yet people today have grown accustomed to being punished with fines or imprisonment when they have neither harmed anyone nor violated anyone's rights.

Multitudes receive punishment every year for such things as driving without a seatbelt, carrying a weapon without a permit, disciplining their children according to biblical standards, going a few miles over an arbitrary speed limit, having an expired inspection sticker, driving without car insurance, driving with an expired driver's license, and for not having health insurance, thanks to ObamaCare. Who have they harmed? Whose property has been damaged? Whose rights have they violated?

Some believe that without these **color of law** dictates, there would be chaos, but it wasn't that long ago when none of these existed and people got along just fine. Even so, some still believe they are necessary because they keep us safe and maintain order by forcing irresponsible people to become responsible citizens.

Whether these so-called "laws" keep us safe is debatable, but one thing is sure; they destroy freedom by penalizing people who have not harmed anyone or their property. Federal, state, county, and local governments create thousands of codes, rules, regulations and statutes every year that impose stiff penalties on people for violating nothing more than petty, bureaucratic, revenue-generating minutia. These actions are done in violation of the Constitution and the first sentence of **<u>Romans 13:3</u>**, *"...for rulers are not a cause of fear for good behavior, but for evil."*

The cost of incarcerating people on these arbitrary statutory infractions created by bureaucrats is alarming.

> "Stated in financial terms, as of 2006, the federal government and all state governments spent a staggering $109 billion annually on feeding, clothing, and confining imprisoned adults, as well as nearly $98 billion on police services and $47 billion on prosecutions." [123]

> "Although America has approximately 5 percent of the global population, 25 percent of the world's prisoners reside here ... only a small fraction of the federal government's criminal code can be considered truly legitimate, and it is the government, and not the individual it prosecutes, that is guilty of the greater unlawful conduct. It is high time that we utilize the criminal law for its one and only purpose: To safeguard our liberties, not restrain them." [124]

People should be able to go about their business without any fear of punitive action from the government as long as they haven't infringed on anyone else's rights or property.

WHAT IS BAD BEHAVIOR?

> *You shall not murder. 14) You shall not commit adultery. 15) You shall not steal. 16) You shall not bear false witness against your neighbor.* **_Exodus 20:13-16_**

---

[123] *Bureau of Justice Statistics*, "Key Facts at a Glance; Direct Expenditures by Criminal Justice Function", *1982-2006.*

[124] Judge Andrew P. Napolitano, *It Is Dangerous To Be Right When the Government Is Wrong*, p. 241

You shall not steal, nor deal falsely, nor lie to one another. 12) You shall not swear falsely by My name, so as to profane the name of your God; I am the LORD. 13) You shall not oppress your neighbor. **Leviticus 19:11-13**

You shall not go about as a slanderer among your people, and you are not to act against the life of your neighbor. **Leviticus 19:16**

You shall not take vengeance. **Leviticus 19:18**

...being filled with all unrighteousness, wickedness, greed, evil; full of envy, murder, strife, deceit, malice. **Romans 1:29-32**

Bad behavior is easy to identify, so there should be no confusion about what kind of behavior rulers should praise and what kind they should punish.

Romans 13:3 (b)

Do you want to have no fear of authority? Do what is good, and you will have praise from the same...

When a person treats others the way he would like to be treated, he should have nothing to fear from governing authorities. God has given man a conscience, but if he lacks discernment and/or rejects principles of right and wrong, he should be afraid because God has given rulers the responsibility of punishing wrongdoers.

ROMANS 13:4   MINISTERS OF GOD FOR GOOD

(a) For it is a minister of God to you for good. (b) But if you do what is evil, be afraid; for it does not bear the sword for nothing; (c) for it is a minister of God, an avenger who brings wrath upon the one who practices evil.

The word *"****minister****"* is a noun referring to a minister, servant, or deacon. The phrase can be translated either way as shown below:

For he is [keeps on being] *a **minister*** [servant] ***of God to you for good.***

For it [government] *is* [keeps on being] *a **minister*** [servant] ***of God to you for good.***

This verse makes a sharp distinction between governing authorities who have God's approval and those who do not. Unjust rulers are not legitimate; they are not God's ministers for they operate without His authorization. They are ministers of Satan for evil.

God never designed government to be a minister of evil. When it becomes evil, it no longer functions as a servant of God for good but as a servant of Satan for evil, and we are not required to submit to Satan's servants but to resist them.

Two verses tell us to resist the devil:

> *Submit therefore to God. Resist the devil and he will flee from you.* **James 4:7**

> *Be of sober spirit, be on the alert. Your adversary, the devil, prowls about like a roaring lion, seeking someone to devour. 9) But resist him, firm in your faith...* **1 Peter 5:8-9**

Since we are commanded to resist Satan, then we must certainly be allowed to resist those who have become his servants.

God designed the structure of civil authorities in the human realm to be subject to Himself, so they must rule according to His just and righteous standards.

By me, kings reign and rulers decree justice. 16) By me, princes rule and nobles, <u>all who judge rightly</u>. **Proverbs 8:15-16**

He who rules over men must be just, ruling in the fear of God. (NKJV) **2 Samuel 23:3**

Notice that only rulers who decree justice and judge rightly have God's authorization backing their decisions.

But we know that the Law is good if one uses it lawfully.... **1 Timothy 1:8**

Governing authorities who take advantage of people by twisting and distorting the law in order to benefit themselves are said to be acting "under the color of law". They come under the condemnation of God and lose the lawful authority they once had.

Quote from Rev. Jonathan Mayhew's sermons: "The king is as much bound by his oath not to infringe the legal rights of the people, as the people are bound to yield subjection to him. From whence it follows that as soon as the prince sets himself above the law, he loses the king in the tyrant. He does, to all intents and purposes, un-king himself." [125]

Romans 13:4 (b)

But if you do what is evil, be afraid; for it does not bear the sword for nothing....

---

[125] Federer, W. J. (2001). *Great Quotations: A Collection of Passages, Phrases, and Quotations Influencing Early and Modern World History,* Referenced according to their Sources in Literature, Memoirs, Letters, Governmental Documents, Speeches, Charters, Court Decisions and Constitutions. St. Louis, MO: AmeriSearch.

This is a warning to anyone who defies God and His servants responsible for enforcing His righteous standards. The phrase, **"*for it* (he) *does not bear the sword for nothing*",** is a clear reference to capital punishment. Executing criminals for capital crimes such as murder is a universal, biblical principle that should be practiced by all nations today. The Bible is clear on this issue.

> *Whoever sheds man's blood, by man his blood shall be shed, for in the image of God He made man.* **Genesis 9:6**

> *He who strikes a man so that he dies shall surely be put to death.* **Exodus 21:12**

> *And if a man takes the life of any human being, he shall surely be put to death.* **Leviticus 24:17**

William Matheson said the following in an article in the Westminster Theological Journal called, *"Justice in the Social Order"*:

> "When it is written that the ruler 'beareth not the sword in vain', his authority to exercise physical force to restrain evildoers is clearly intended. Therefore he is to be feared by evildoers. It is also indicated that in resisting evildoers his authority extends to the power over life itself. In other words, governments have power from God to resist evildoers to the death... It is specifically an authority limited to the necessity for maintaining justice within and without any government's domain. *No government can have any right from God to exercise this authority in the cause of evil or injustice.* [Emphasis added]" [126]

---

[126] William Matheson. "Justice in the Social Order", *Westminster Theological Journal,* Volume 08. 1945 (2) (145–146). Philadelphia: Westminster Theological Seminary.

Romans 13:4 (c)

***...for it is a minister of God,** an avenger who brings wrath upon the one who practices evil.*

This can be translated either:

For *it* is a minister of God... or
For *he* is a minister of God...

Both are accurate translations.

For the second time in <u>verse 4</u> we are reminded that those in government are the servants of God. A servant is under obligation to render obedience to the one who has authority over him. He is not free to do whatever he wants. He is required to follow God's righteous standards in administering his office by being ***"...an avenger who brings wrath upon the one who practices evil."***

> "For God has delegated to civil magistrates in place of parents the right to punish evildoers." [127]

It is very important to understand what this verse does **NOT** say. It does not say civil magistrates have the authority or sanction from God to bring wrath on the one who does good. NEVER! When rulers bring wrath upon those who do right, they lose their right to govern.

On January 30, 1750, a phenomenal colonial pastor named Jonathan Mayhew delivered a sermon on <u>Romans 13:1-7</u>. Following is a quote from that sermon:

> "The apostle's [Paul] doctrine... may be summed up in the following observations, viz.: That the end of

---

[127] Martin Luther, *Luther's Cat. Writings*, p. 79.

> magistracy is the good of civil society... That civil rulers, as such, are the ordinance and ministers of God; it being by His permission and providence that any bear rule and agreeable to His will that there should be some persons vested with authority in society, for the well-being of it... It is obvious then, in general, that the civil rulers whom the apostle speaks of, and obedience to whom he presses upon Christians as a duty, are good rulers, such as are, in the exercise of their office and power, benefactors to society...." [128]

Fair and impartial governing officials are to be obeyed because they submit to God's authority, but unjust rulers can be disobeyed because they forfeit their authority when they defy God.

> "Since all authority comes from God, it should be that all valid governments be based on God's laws. When officers or judges in authority do not exercise that authority for its designed purpose, the obligation to them would consequently cease to exist. This was the basis of the American Revolution in 1776." [129]

There are verses in 1 Peter 2 that are similar to the ones in Romans 13. They also refer to rulers who function as God's emissaries, who punish evildoers and praise those who do right. It is to this type of ruler that submission is due.

---

[128] Jonathan Mayhew, January 30, 1750, in the sermon "A Discourse Concerning Unlimited Submission and Non-resistance to the Higher Powers, etc., etc.", *The Annals of America,* 20 vols. (Chicago, IL: *Encyclopedia Britannica,* 1968), Vol. 1, pp. 482-483.

[129] Charles A. Weisman, *A Handbook of Biblical Law,* 1991 Weisman Publications, p. 66.

Submit yourselves for the Lord's sake to every human institution, whether to a king as the one in authority14) or to governors as sent by him [God] for the punishment of evildoers and the praise of those who do right. **1 Peter 2:13-14**

The Apostle Peter, like the Apostle Paul, limits the range of governmental authority to that of punishing evildoers but not the innocent. Verse 14 makes it clear that submission is required when the one in authority is acting as a servant of God on God's behalf and not on his own.

"*Every human institution*" includes the differing systems and levels of authority that God delegated to governing officials. Peter gave two examples, kings and governors. Obviously, Peter was referring to legitimate institutions, not tyrannical ones as they are not "sent from God"; indeed, they defy Him.

The abusive power they wield is not delegated to them by God otherwise God would be the instigator of sin. God commands us to submit to legitimate, lawful authority, but to say that our submission must be "unconditional" is going too far. **We owe unconditional submission to God only, never to man.**

For such is the will of God that by doing right you may silence the ignorance of foolish men.16) Act as free men, and do not use your freedom as a covering for evil, but use it as bond slaves of God.
1 Peter 2:15-16

"This section of Peter's argument leads many to believe that the organized persecution through oppressive Roman laws either had not begun or had not yet reached the provinces of Asia Minor.

Christians were then facing lies and verbal abuse, not torture and death. Christians were still enjoying the protection of a legal system which commended those who obeyed the law. So a believer's best defense against slanderous criticism was good behavior." [130]

This verse does not say nor does it imply that we are required to be bondslaves of government. Submission to lawful authority does not negate Christian liberty.

Honor all men; love the brotherhood, fear God, honor the king. **1 Peter 2:17**

We are to show proper respect to all men, especially those who rule such as kings or presidents. The position demands respect even if the person holding that position does not.

Servants, be submissive to your masters with all respect, not only to those who are good and gentle, but also to those who are unreasonable. **1 Peter 2:18**

The word "servants" is translated from a Greek word that is often translated "slave". It is important to note that this verse refers to a slave/master relationship, not a government/citizen relationship. Governing authorities are not our masters and we are not their slaves. Slavery existed when this was written and had a set of rules and standards that were different from those that applied to free men.

Verse 18 required slaves to submit to their masters even if they were "unreasonable"; it doesn't say, "even

---

[130] Walvoord, J. F., Zuck, R. B., & Dallas Theological Seminary. (1985). *The Bible Knowledge Commentary: An Exposition of the Scriptures* (1 Peter 2:13-15). Wheaton, IL: Victor Books.

if they were abusive". There is a big difference between being unreasonable and being a bully. God does not require submission to abuse.

Slaves who had accepted the gospel were not to disobey or flee from their masters once they became Christians. They could lawfully gain their freedom if the Lord opened that door for them. But God can use Christians who are willing to serve Him regardless of their status, whether slaves or free.

> *Let each man remain in that condition in which he was called. 21) Were you called while a slave? Do not worry about it; but if you are able also to become free, rather do that. 22) For he who was called in the Lord while a slave, is the Lord's freedman; likewise he who was called while free, is Christ's slave. 23) You were bought with a price; do not become slaves of men. 24) Brethren, let each man remain with God in that condition in which he was called.*
> **1 Corinthians 7:20-24**

Paul's epistle to the Galatians addressed the issue of freedom:

> *It was for freedom that Christ set us free; therefore keep standing firm and do not be subject again to a yoke of slavery.* **Galatians 5:1**

The context of this verse relates to believers who were no longer under the Mosaic Law, yet they were still trying to conform to its legal demands, a practice that is called **legalism**. This verse confirms the importance of freedom in the life of Christians.

God delegated His authority to rulers to establish righteousness, not wickedness. When they become tyrants and practice evil, He strongly condemns them.

> *It is an abomination for kings to commit wickedness, for a* [legitimate] *throne is established on righteousness.* **Proverbs 16:12**

> *He who justifies the wicked, and he who condemns the righteous, both of them alike are an abomination to the LORD.* **Proverbs 17:15**

Judges 9:1-57 says that Government officers who committed conspiracy, treachery, or murder were to be put to death. The problem today is that many people have become so dumbed down that they think the government actually has the *right* to impose unjust, freedom-destroying, unconstitutional laws on them and they don't have the right to disobey them. Just let that horrible fact sink in for a moment. How could that happen? This mindset has developed over a long period of time as the people acquiesced to the incremental encroachments of a government that knows no limits.

> "Arbitrary power...must be introduced by slow degrees, and as it were, step by step, lest the people should see it approach."
> ~ Lord Chesterfield ~

> "America was founded on the common law model that assumes there is a higher law than any government's law. But over the decades this model has been gradually subverted and replaced by Roman Law... Justice is whatever lawmakers say it is." [131]

The idea of limiting civil authority is nothing new. The men who founded our country were very intent on

---

[131] Richard J. Maybury, *Ancient Rome, How It Affects You Today,* 2004, Bluestocking Press, p. 33.

living according to the mandates of the Bible, and they certainly believed that God gives only limited authority to civil government.

"The source most often cited by the founding fathers was the Bible, which accounted for 34 percent of all citations." [132]

"Wheresoever the General Government assumes un-delegated powers, its acts are un-authoritative, void, and of no force." [133]

ROMANS 13:5   SUBMIT FOR CONSCIENCE SAKE

Wherefore it is necessary to be in subjection, not only because of wrath but also for conscience sake.

Conscience has already been covered to some extent on pages 91-106 and will continue in the study of this verse. Keep in mind that the context in which these verses were written refers to a government operating properly as a minister of God for good, therefore our submission is required.

Fear of punishment or reprisals from governing authorities for disobedience is not the only reason we should submit. This may be the reason criminals submit, but we submit to just laws because the Scriptures and our conscience tell us it is the right thing to do.

---

[132] John Eidsmoe, *Christianity and the Constitution,* p. 51.

[133] Tom Rose, "Reconstruction and the American Republic", *Christianity and Civilization,* Geneva Divinity School Press, 1983, p. 296.

OBEYING CONSCIENCE

However, the Scriptures and our conscience sometimes tell us that submitting is the wrong thing to do. In those cases, our conscience motivates us to disobey laws that go against our faith and God-given rights.

> "Paul makes it clear that our submission to civil authority must be predicated on more than fear of governmental retaliation. Notice, he said, 'Wherefore ye must needs be subject, not only for wrath, but also for conscience sake,' meaning our obedience to civil authority is more than just 'because they said so'. It is also a matter of conscience... This means we must think and reason for ourselves regarding the justness and rightness of our government's laws. Obedience is not automatic or robotic. It is a result of both rational deliberation and moral approbation." [134]

We are to do good works and do what is right in order to please God. Our own conscience should restrain us from doing evil and motivate us to do what is right. It is impossible for anyone to live in peace and happiness while going against his conscience. The Colonists understood this which is the reason they could no longer continue to tolerate tyranny.

Remember the battle cry of America's War for Independence in 1776? *"Resistance to tyranny is obedience to God."* They could no longer submit to tyranny and still be at peace with God or their conscience, so they came up with this phrase that reflects their reason for declaring independence.

Some may say that since the battle cry is not found in the Bible, it is not biblical.

---

[134] Chuck Baldwin, "Romans 13 Revisited", Feb.27, 2009, *NewsWithAView.Com*

Well, the phrase may not be found there, but the principle certainly is. The numerous examples of people who resisted tyranny and were blessed by God will be covered in chapter 10.

> "Contextual analysis reveals: Romans 13:1-7 places an emphasis upon the believer's obedience in accord with his conscience. Romans 14:23 establishes the fact that if a believer does anything that violates his conscience, it is a sin. Therefore, it is a sin for a believer to obey a governmental mandate (i.e. law) that violates the moral norms and standards of his conscience. When a believer understands right and wrong, when they do not do what is right, it is a sin of omission." [135]

Therefore, to one who knows the right thing to do, and does not do it, to him it is sin. **James 4:17**

> "'Rebellion against tyrants is obedience to God' is certainly biblical. It is clearly taught 1 Kings 12:1-24, and this biblical principle speaks clearly to Christians today who are concerned about the growth of an anti-Christian absolute State in Washington D.C." [136]

The following is an example of what happens to people when they ignore their own conscience and obey every law no matter how unjust or evil it may be.

---

[135] John K. Eichmann, *Grace Military Ministries Bible Study Newsletter*, p. 7 [emphasis in original].

[136] Tom Rose, "Reconstruction and the American Republic", *Christianity and Civilization*, Geneva Divinity School Press, 1983, p. 295.

THE NUREMBERG TRIALS

Both God and man hold us accountable when we ignore our conscience and submit to evil. Good examples of this are the 1945 Nuremberg Trials where war criminals were tried for committing heinous crimes against humanity. Every one of the defendants had the same defense. Their plea was "Not guilty" because they were merely following orders. They committed atrocities because they refused to disobey the evil authority over them.

They obeyed orders without question, believing that no one has the right to choose which orders or laws they will obey or not obey. The majority of the war criminals were executed because the court realized that **the authority of our own conscience supersedes the authority of those over us.**

The court's verdict was correct because it was based on the right premise. When there is a clash between one's conscience and those in authority, it is the conscience that should be followed. We are all responsible to God for the choices and decisions we make regardless of what those in authority may say. People have the right to disobey unjust laws and the dictates of the state when compliance would cause them to violate their own conscience.

Of course, this does not suggest that we should refuse to submit to injustice in trivial matters. Probably, the most prudent thing to do when you get a speeding ticket, even though you weren't speeding, is to either pay the fine or exercise your right to represent yourself in court, then move on. This principle has been pointed out on page 101 describing how the Declaration of Independence addressed this very issue.

Our goal as Christians is not to bring about a perfect government. We know that is not possible until our Lord returns to earth to set up His millennial kingdom. No government has ever been administered perfectly, and people should recognize that they must abide by certain minor decisions made by the state with which they do not agree.

However, when the state arrogates powers to itself God did not delegate, when it violates fundamental rights of the people, when it disregards the Constitution, when it becomes a minister of Satan for evil, then people have the right to do what is necessary to secure their freedom.

It is instructive to notice what Paul said right before he wrote Romans 13. He concluded chapter twelve with the following:

> *Do not be overcome by evil, but overcome evil with good.* **Romans 12:21**

We have two direct commands here. How can we obey them if we are not allowed to resist the evil dictates of the State?

Not seeking revenge and not repaying evil with evil is good. However, complying with evil is not good, nor is it pleasing to the Lord. There are circumstances where God expects us to endure undeserved suffering without retaliation, but He does not require us to voluntarily yield to the cruelty of a bully or the ruthlessness of a tyrant.

Example: If an employee is unjustly fired, he has the right to seek redress by lawful means to get his job back or to receive compensation. But if that is unsuccessful, he has no right to retaliate, to try to damage the business, or to hurt anyone associated with it. He should put the issue in the Lord's hands and move on.

However, he would have the right to resist any attempts of the business to blacklist him, withhold wages owed him, or tarnish his name and reputation.

> *For it is better, if God should will it so, that you suffer for doing what is right rather than for doing what is wrong.* **1 Peter 3:17**

Good judgment must be used when one refuses to tolerate tyranny. It can be risky and it should be done only after prayer and careful consideration has been made as to the proper time and way to proceed.

> *Since the word of the king is authoritative, who will say to him, "What are you doing?" 5) He who keeps a royal command experiences no trouble, for a wise heart knows the proper time and procedure. 6) For there is a proper time and procedure for every delight, though a man's trouble is heavy upon him.* **Ecclesiastes 8:4-6**

We should never resist abusive authority with defiance or anger. We should be humble and respectful, but resolved that we will not allow anyone to ignore our God-given rights or force us to comply with evil. What should the men that were on trial at Nuremberg have done to avoid being tried for war crimes? They should have disobeyed their superior officers' illegitimate, immoral commands and obeyed their conscience instead.

Refusing to resist evil leaders can be very costly.

AN EVIL KING NOT RESISTED

God is against those who oppress others, Isa. 10:1, Mica 2:1, so shouldn't we be against them as well? Jesus said, "He who is not with Me is against Me", Matt. 12:30. There is no neutral ground relating to Jesus, nor is there neutrality relating to good and evil. When we do nothing to resist those who oppress us and others, we condone their evil deeds and come under God's judgment. It is the duty of every person to defend their own rights as well as the rights of those who are unable to defend themselves.

The Bible records what happens to people who do not resist an abusively evil ruler. God holds the people responsible for doing nothing to resist the wicked actions of their king.

> *And I* [God] *shall make them* [the people] *an object of horror among all the kingdoms of the earth because of Manasseh, the son of Hezekiah, the king of Judah, for what he did in Jerusalem.* **Jeremiah 15:4**

This is a very interesting verse because it highlights the danger of not resisting an authority that is evil. Manasseh was arguably the most wicked king Judah ever had. Notice that God held the people responsible for what the king did. Why? Surely it could be for only one reason: they failed to resist him. They went along with the idolatry, the daily executions, the shocking immorality, and the human sacrifices.

Throughout the ages, men have had to decide whether to submit to evil and simply do as they were told or to resist and do what was right. God demonstrates how He holds His people responsible for submitting to evil instead of resisting it in Jeremiah 15:4.

"Evil has no authority apart from human consent. We are the products of our own decisions. We are constantly assigning authority to evil people who represent the cosmic [worldly] system. This is how dictators become oppressors of the people. This explains the rise of terror in the French Revolution, as well as the rise of Lenin, Stalin, and Hitler." [137]

Tyrants are only as powerful as people allow them to be. When their encroachments are not resisted, they become more emboldened.

Apathy causes people to think that an appalling situation will get better by doing nothing about it. That attitude leads to slavery. Freedom must be maintained. It has already died when people do nothing more than merely hope for the best as despots continue to go about oppressing them.

"I often wonder whether we do not rest our hopes too much upon constitutions, upon law and upon courts. These are false hopes, believe me, these are false hopes. Liberty lies in the hearts of men and women; when it dies there, no constitution, no law, no court can save it; No constitution, no law, no court can even do much to help it. While it lies there it needs no constitution, no law, no courts to save it." [138]

ROMANS 13:6   PAYING TAXES

(a) For because of this you also pay taxes, (b) for rulers are <u>servants</u> of God, devoting themselves to this very thing.

---

[137] R.B. Thieme Jr. Notes on "Authority", point 8d.

[138] Judge Learned Hand (1872-1961), Judge, U.S. Court of Appeals, http://quotes.libertytree.ca/quote_blog/Learned.Hand Quote. B58E

The authority structure of government over citizens requires financial support, therefore it is our duty to pay the taxes that we owe. So the context suggests that taxes are paid for the support of those who are servants of God who devote their time and energies to administer government. It is only right that those in government be supported by those they serve since their time is spent administering the affairs of government for us all.

Governing authorities are to be supported by taxes from the people for the same reason the tribe of Levi, the priestly tribe, was supported by the other tribes of Israel. The priests devoted themselves to serving the people and therefore could not provide for their own needs. So they received support from those they served.

> *For the Scripture says, "you shall not muzzle the ox while he is threshing," and "The laborer is worthy of his wages".* **1 Timothy 5:18**

Unfortunately, many politicians today are more interested in serving themselves than in serving God or the people.

Levying taxes is a serious business. Many wars have been fought over taxes. It certainly was an issue in the 1st War of Independence, aka. the "Revolutionary War" as well as the 2nd War of Independence, aka. The "Civil War".

> "To compel a man to subsidize with his taxes the propagation of ideas which he disbelieves and abhors is sinful and tyrannical."
> *~ Thomas Jefferson ~*

The tax system Americans must endure is beyond horrendous. It is evil. There are 73,954 pages in the Internal Revenue Service Code. The tax burden is so heavy on most families that the husband's income cannot support it alone, so wives must go to work in order to cover the overwhelming tax obligation.

> "The Original Sin which brought us to the brink of bankruptcy and dictatorship was the Federal Income Tax Amendment and its illegitimate child, Federal Aid." [139]

Our convoluted, progressive income tax system is a disgrace. No one should be taxed at a higher rate because they have a higher income than others. The Lord's assessment on the Israelites was simple, fair, and non-progressive.

> *Everyone who is numbered, from twenty years old and over, shall give the contribution to the LORD. 15) "The rich shall not pay more, and the poor shall not pay less than the half shekel, when you give the contribution to the LORD.* **Exodus 30:14-15**

Americans are forced to pay taxes that are unbiblical, an example being the inheritance tax. The government has no right to any of the inheritance that parents or grandparents pass down to their children or grandchildren. Didn't these parents already pay taxes on their earnings?

> *The prince shall not take from the people's inheritance, thrusting them out of their possession; he shall give his sons inheritance from his own possession so that My people will not be scattered, anyone from his possession.* **Ezekiel 46:18**

---

[139] Tom Anderson, *http://quotes.liberty-tree.ca/DailyQuotes*

People have a natural right to pass on their full inheritance to their heirs without anyone, including the government, interfering with their personal and private transactions.

Government has no right to take the hard-earned money from people who have earned it and to give it to someone else through taxation.

> "The federal government takes money from the people who have earned it and gives it to the people who have not earned it. When this is done privately, we call it theft. When it is done by the federal government, we use euphemisms to describe it, such as "income transfers" or "wealth redistribution" or social welfare payments." [140]

A constant flow of money is required to feed the reckless spending of our Congress. To support this insatiable addiction, they raise taxes and print more money, but even these measures fail to supply enough funds so they borrow the rest. The amount they have borrowed presently stands at about 17 trillion dollars. The printing presses must run around the clock just to print the billions needed to pay the interest on what they borrowed.

This kind of activity was called "legal plunder" by Federic Bastiat, the French economist and statesman who authored the book, *The Law,* in 1850. He excoriated rulers who enriched themselves at the expense of the common people. Now, let's continue with verse 6.

---

[140] Brian Farmer, "Is Soaking the Rich the Right Answer?" *The New American,* March 4, 2013, p. 19.

Romans 13:6 (b)   SUPPORT FOR DEVOTED SERVANTS OF GOD

...for rulers are <u>servants</u> of God, devoting themselves to this very thing. NASV

...for rulers are <u>ministers</u> of God... KJV

Whether they are called "servants" or "ministers", the context consistently refers to legitimate rulers who are servants of God for good and servants of the people as well. Everything is predicated upon that fact.

"**<u>Servants</u> of God...**" is a different Greek word than the one that was translated **"minister"** in <u>verse 4</u>. The word there related to governing authorities in their relationship to God while here, the word relates more to their function as public servants of the people.

This specific Greek word translated "ministers" or "servants" was used for a purpose. It is God's way of telling us that legitimate civil rulers are servants of God as well as servants of the people. They are not lords or sovereigns.

...devoting themselves to this very thing.

Rulers serve God by serving the people. They are His agents and are to carry out the duty of praising those who do what is right and punishing those who do evil.

RENDER UNTO CAESAR...WHO IS CAESAR?

<u>ROMANS 13:7</u>

Render to all what is due them: tax to whom tax is due; custom to whom custom; fear to whom fear; honor to whom honor.

Who determines how much tax each individual owes? With our progressive income tax system, each individual is expected to try to determine what is due using incomprehensible tax codes and complicated forms or to hire someone to figure it out for them and hope they get it right. Then each individual is required to sign those forms under penalty of perjury. The unfairness of such a system should be obvious.

The Pharisees tried to incriminate Jesus by asking Him whether it was lawful to pay taxes to Caesar or not. Our Lord gave the following answer:

> *Render to Caesar the things that are Caesar's; and to God the things that are God's."* **Matthew 22:21**

Most people mistakenly think this means to render to Caesar anything he demands; and to God, whatever is left.

But such an interpretation is certainly not what Jesus said nor is it what He meant. He was explaining that we have responsibility to God and to the state as well. The Apostle Paul used the same Greek word in Romans 13:7, with the same meaning, "to render", as Matthew used in the verse above.

The first question that must be answered is, "Who is Caesar in the United States?" The answer is of course, NO ONE. We don't have a Caesar; no person has absolute authority in our country. We do have an absolute authority but it isn't a "who", it's a "what". It's the Constitution and the Bill of Rights. Everyone is required to submit to them because, excluding the natural law of God, they are the highest laws in the land.

Our President is not Caesar, no Senator is Caesar, nor is any Congressman Caesar!

They all take an oath to submit to the Constitution. They cannot lawfully ignore it, God, or the people, and yet most citizens let them get by with breaking their oaths with impunity and doing whatever they please.

Jesus was not specific about what one owes to Caesar, but we know for certain that He would not leave that decision up to Caesar because it would enable him to declare that everything we own belongs to him. By the way, that is the essence of Communism: everything, including the people, belong to the STATE.

> "Surely the king doesn't get to touch his finger to any ol' thing he pleases and say, 'Mine!' It would be the height, or maybe the depth, of foolishness to agree to 'render unto Caesar' and then give Caesar the privilege of declaring what is his... Nowhere in God's book are kings allowed to act like that (although they do so, shaking their fists at God.) And so, since God doesn't allow it, righteousness does not demand it of you! What the righteousness of God, as defined in His Book, the Bible, demands from cover to cover from the people of God is that they stand firm in the evil day." [141]

We are to pay fair, legitimate, lawful taxes that are necessary for our government to function within the confines of the Constitution and biblical principles. That is what is to be rendered to Caesar. What most people don't realize is that alcohol, tobacco, firearms and import taxes alone provide more than enough money to run the government efficiently when it operates within the confines of the Constitution.

---

[141] Runyan, Gordan, *Resistance to Tyrants: Romans 13 and the Christian Duty to Oppose Wicked Rulers* (p. 46-47).

"Unjust government is not God's deacon [minister], and therefore has no legitimate right to the money earned by God's people, even if it seems to be going through the right motions." *Ibid*, p. 36

Samuel Adams described their situation back in 1771 that happens to describe our situation today: "The people are paying the unrighteous tribute in hopes that the nation will at length revert to justice. But before that time comes, it is to be feared they will be so accustomed to bondage, as to forget they were ever free."

...*custom* to whom *custom*...refers to a toll or a custom; i.e. an indirect tax on goods.

...*fear* to whom *fear*...from the Greek word PHOBOS can mean fear, reverence, respect, or honor. We are to respect those to whom respect is due.

...*honor* to whom *honor*... can mean esteem, respect, honor, or reverence.

The positions of authority that people hold should be respected. Governing authorities who are servants of God for good should be supported by the people they serve. They deserve respect and honor for being good servants of God and the people. But, governing authorities who are not servants of God who break their oaths of office deserve no respect, honor, support or submission.

Believers are to be balanced in their thinking and should have a humble, respectful attitude toward everyone, especially those who hold positions of authority. However, recognition of one's authority does not require absolute obeisance, especially when the person is a dishonorable scoundrel who harasses or threatens people.

"Those who hold no merit of honor hold no divine protection from God and no entitlement of submission. At some point, the souls under a particular regime may determine to remove such dishonorable rulers... and such would be their God-given right and duty." [142]

---

[142] Timothy Baldwin and Chuck Baldwin, *Romans 13, The True Meaning of Submission,* p. 134.

CHAPTER 8

OBJECTIONS TO RESISTING TYRANNY

1) CHRISTIANS SHOULD AVOID WORLDLY ENTANGLEMENTS

Some say Christians should not get entangled in the affairs of the world. Does that mean that Christians should not get involved in doing what it takes to keep and maintain their liberty? They shouldn't join the military, vote, or hold office? Does it mean they should not get involved in politics or speak out or protest against immoral or unjust laws and policies of a corrupt government?

Does it mean they do not have the same right other Americans have to exercise their faith, express their views, assemble together, or petition the government?

Were Pastor Jonas Clark and the Christian men from his church he led onto Lexington Green wrong to entangle themselves in the affairs of the world when they opposed the British? Should they have done nothing to stop the soldiers from taking their only means to defend themselves against tyranny? If Christians don't take a stand for righteousness and justice, who will? What would unbelievers think if Christians dropped the struggle for freedom entirely on their shoulders? More importantly, what would God think of them?

Some use Scriptures that focus on the spiritual aspects of our conflicts in life, such as Ephesians chapter six, as an excuse for not getting involved in the affairs of this world. Their idea is that our struggle should only be against the unseen angelic forces and not against tyrants in the human realm.

They use the following verse to support their viewpoint:

> *For our struggle is not against flesh and blood, but against the rulers, against the powers, against the world forces of this darkness, against the spiritual forces of wickedness in the heavenly places. 13) Therefore, take up the full armor of God, so that you will be able to resist in the evil day, and having done everything, to stand firm. 14) Stand firm therefore....* **Ephesians 6:12-14**

Yes, we are indeed involved in an unseen spiritual struggle known as the "angelic conflict". It started when Satan rebelled against God in eternity past before man was created and continues today. It is part of the spiritual dimension of our struggles in this life.

Evil people are controlled or influenced by angelic forces and rulers of darkness. In that sense, our battle is not against flesh and blood. However, humans are certainly a part of the ongoing angelic conflict because fallen angels use them to achieve their satanic goals. We must stay spiritually strong, wearing the full armor of God, as described in Ephesians 6:14-17, in order to defeat wicked people and the fallen angels who control them.

Ephesians 6:13 tells us to put on the full armor of God so that we can "resist in the evil day". Do we live in an evil day? Yes. Should we resist? Yes, but how can we if we are not allowed to resist the very tyrants who carry out the evil promoted by fallen angels?

*Therefore, take up the full armor of God, so that you will be able to resist in the evil day, and having done everything, to **stand firm**. 14) **Stand firm** therefore….*
Ephesians 6:13-14

"Stand firm" is used twice in these verses. In verse 14 it is a verb in the imperative mood which means it is a command requiring us to act. It entails more than just praying and acquiring spiritual knowledge. While those are both important, it is the application of that knowledge toward people and circumstances that God is commanding. The point is, our job is to resist evil by utilizing the spiritual assets and discernment God has given us so that we can stand firm for righteousness.

Open your mouth for the mute, for the rights of all the unfortunate. 9) Open your mouth, judge righteously, and defend the rights of the afflicted and needy.
Proverbs 31:8-9

Learn to do good; seek justice, reprove the ruthless, defend the orphan, plead for the widow. **Isaiah 1:17**

Jesus was certainly involved in the struggles of life; He healed the sick, fed the hungry, and rebuked unjust leaders who took advantage of people. He reprimanded the Pharisees to their faces and called them "a brood of vipers", Matt. 12:34, and "hypocrites", and "white washed tombstones" which on the outside appear beautiful, but inside they are "full of dead men's bones and all uncleanness," Matthew 23:27.

2) WE SHOULD FOLLOW THE FIRST CENTURY CHRISTIANS' EXAMPLE

Some people point out the believers of the first century who submitted to the Roman Empire's oppression and abuse as an example that we should follow. They did not fight for their liberty.

First of all, one might question the wisdom of making the behavior of first century Christians the standard to follow rather than the commandments and principles of Scripture. For example, no one should follow the deplorable behavior of the Corinthian believers of the first century that ran the gamut from legalism to licentiousness.

Furthermore, first century Christians did not have the advantage of the completed canon of Scripture that we enjoy today to guide their behavior. We also have the benefit of analyzing the history of the church for the past two thousand years to see what happens to people who voluntarily submit to tyranny.

Another difficulty arises when trying to equate their relationship to government with ours. Their circumstances were so different from ours that they can hardly be compared.

The Jews were a conquered people under the absolute domination of Rome. They had no contract, constitution, or voice as to the kind of treatment they received from their conquerors. Of course, our situation is very different. We are not an occupied country; we have a Bill of Rights and a constitution designed to keep our rulers in check. We have a voice in who will govern us when we cast our vote at the ballot box. The Jews had no say as to who ruled over them, and few, if any, official options were available to them to resist their rulers when they acted unjustly.

3) PASTORS SHOULD STAY OUT OF POLITICS

In modern America, most pastors have failed to teach biblical principles concerning freedom and government to their congregations. The result has been predictable. We have become a biblically and historically illiterate society that lacks the knowledge and courage to take our freedoms back.

The Christian community has remained silent and has willingly acquiesced to the ever-growing power and unconstitutional acts of the federal and state governments. Because of our abysmal ignorance, misplaced loyalty and fear, an aggressive, humanistic state has developed that is poised to crush any type of dissent.

It is imperative that pastors teach their congregations that the Bible does not require them to tolerate the curtailment of their freedoms, even when governmental limitations come incrementally, in small doses.

> "Eternal vigilance is the price of liberty."
> *~Thomas Jefferson~*

Ultimately, the history of Western civilization is the history of Christians struggling against an unlawful, dominating state and the anti-Christian policies that undergird it.

Pastors are often criticized for being too political when they speak out about political issues and especially if they censure policies or people involved in government. Shouldn't pastors, or anyone else for that matter, be free to condemn evil wherever it exists? When did pastors who denounce the corrupt practices of oppressive leaders fall into disrepute?

"Often governments may think they have a right to that which should belong to God. That would be an intolerable usurpation and it is the job of the clergy to be on the side of the people on God's behalf." [143]

Why is it OK for pastors to condemn immorality, abuse, and wrongdoing in business, society, entertainment, education, churches, and the media, but not condemn politicians or government? Why should that be off limits? What chapter and verse in the Bible prohibits pastors from speaking out about the atrocious and deplorable behavior of evil politicians who stealthily strip away our rights?

Many pastors are afraid to confront corrupt officials because they are cowed and intimidated by those in their own congregations. They don't teach the whole council of God because they are afraid of offending someone who might accuse them of being too political, unpatriotic, or disloyal to government.

PASTORS, POLITICS AND THE BLACK-ROBED REGIMENT

Whenever issues relate to morality and justice, it is the role of pastors to address those issues from the pulpit and challenge our political leaders to do the right thing. This has been the tradition of this nation since colonial times, and if it were not for the courage and leadership of the pastors in 1775, we would still be bowing to British royalty.

The British feared no group more than they feared the Colonial pastors. They hated them because they taught

---

[143] Gregory Williams, "Romans 13 & Christ's Clergy Response Teams", *NewsWithViews.com,* 1-21-09.

their congregations the biblical principles of freedom and resistance to tyranny. Writing a little less than a century after the battle of Lexington and Concord, the Rev. William Ware of Cambridge, MA wrote:

> "When the struggle [at Lexington] actually commenced, the people were ready for it, thoroughly acquainted with the reasons on which the duty of resistance was founded, and prepared to discharge the duty at every hazard. No population within the compass of the Colonies were better prepared for the events of the 19th of April [1775], than the people of Lexington...." [144]

America is perishing because most pastors are not teaching their congregations the biblical perspective of freedom as it relates to personal, civil, and religious life. We need more men like Jonas Clark, the Colonial pastor of the church in Lexington who taught the great doctrine of salvation through faith in Jesus Christ as well as the biblical right to resist tyranny.

He prepared his congregation to be ready for whatever challenges came their way because he typically taught four, one-hour sermons each week that amounted to nearly 2,200 sermons during his lifetime. The men of his congregation had the courage to stand their ground alongside him while facing overwhelming odds because they knew their actions were supported by God. The Battle of Lexington should inspire us to stand our ground as well. Jonas Clark was one of the patriot pastors known as the "Black Regiment" or sometimes called the "Black-Robed Regiment" because of the black robes they wore while preaching.

---

[144] *http://www.nordskogpublishing.com/author-Jonas-Clark.shtml*

> "The 'Black Regiment' was a group of patriot-preachers from virtually every protestant denomination located throughout Colonial America at the time of America's fight for independence who courageously preached the biblical principles of liberty and independence. The moniker stems from the tendency of these patriot-preachers to wear long, black robes in their pulpits." [145]

John Adams, himself, declared that the Rev. Dr. Jonathan Mayhew and the Rev. Dr. Samuel Cooper were two of the individuals "most conspicuous, the most ardent, and influential" in the "awakening and revival of American principles and feelings" that led to American independence.

How are Christians going to learn the biblical principles that relate to civil government if their pastors are afraid to address political issues? Pastors should not be intimidated about praising a person or organization worthy of praise nor should they be timid about condemning politicians who betray their oath of office and ignore their responsibility to God and the people they represent.

The history of our country shows that black-robed, regiment pastors were very involved in praising or denouncing the policies and leaders of state.

> "Because the 'Black Regiment' understood the Biblical roles of church and state, and the proper biblical response of the church toward the state, the American republic was born. The clergy of the American Colonies preached freedom from tyranny. The Rev. Samuel West preached that it is just as evil to avoid opposing tyranny as it is to disobey

---

[145] *http://chuckbaldwinlive.com/home/black-regiment*

righteous leaders. Citing Romans chapter 13, Rev. West pointed out that civil magistrates are 'ministers of God' and therefore draw their authority from God's law. He resounded that when the civil magistrate subverts the authority given by God, it is the duty of lesser magistrates to resist them." [146]

Some believe that the principle of separation between church and state should keep pastors from addressing political issues from the pulpit. They mistakenly believe this principle requires Christians to keep their religion inside the church and forbids them from criticizing or interfering in the affairs of the state.

> "[The insertion] ...of the 'Separation between Church and State' doctrine into the fabric of American culture is one of the greatest acts of fraud and deception ever to be perpetrated upon the American people. The doctrine is nothing more than a legal fiction brought into existence only by committing tremendous violence against the founders' original vision for the country." [147]

The Bill of Rights limits the state, not the church. The state is prohibited from establishing a particular religion or denomination to be the official state religion.

> "Congress shall make no law respecting an establishment of religion, or prohibiting the free exercise thereof.... " (Article 1 in the Bill of Rights)

You may notice that the words "church", "state", and "separation" are not even found in the first article of the Bill of Rights which is the one that specifically deals

---

[146] Randy Pope, http://lwhf.com/black_regiment.html

[147] Dr. Andy Woods, *"Darwin, Evolution, and the American Constitution"*, March 2011, p. 64.

with the relationship between government and religion. There have been periods in history when the Catholic Church assumed the state's power which certainly is not biblical. The state has its area of authority and the church has its area.

The state has no authority to tell pastors what they can and cannot preach, nor do pastors have the authority to tell governing officials what to do. However, pastors can teach their congregations the biblical limitations of civil authority and the doctrine of conditional submission. They also have the authority to commend or repudiate the acts and decisions of governing officials from their pulpits.

Christians who stand for righteousness and morality are not a threat to good government; they are a blessing to it. Holding officials to their oath of office and to moral standards is not an act of treachery; it is a patriotic as well as a Christian duty.

On the occasion of the Boston Massacre, March 5, 1774, John Hancock gave an oration in Boston that was printed in five pamphlet editions and widely circulated:

> "Some boast of being 'friends to government': I am a friend to 'righteous' government, to a government founded upon the principles of reason and justice.... I have the most animating confidence that the present noble struggle for liberty will terminate gloriously for America. And let us play the man for our GOD, and for the cities of our GOD; while we are using the means in our power, let us humbly commit our righteous cause to the great LORD of the universe, who loveth righteousness and hateth inequity. And having secured the approbation of our hearts, by a

faithful and unwearied discharge of our duty to our country, let us joyfully leave her important concerns in the hands of HIM who raiseth up and putteth down empires and kingdoms of the world as HE pleases...." [148]

Dr. Wayne House does not see any prohibition in the Scriptures against Christians protesting or denouncing unjust or immoral actions.

"First, at a minimum, Christians, as concerned, responsible citizens, should voice opposition to unjust or immoral actions on the part of government. They can use all lawful forms of opposition and protest, such as the utilization of the freedoms of speech and assembly enjoyed in our country, to write letters, sign petitions, form political lobbies, picket, run for political office, etc., in short, to aggressively engage in the many lawful forms of protest available to us under applicable federal and state law. Biblical support for this function is found in the Old Testament prophets, who regularly denounced the social injustices of their day on the authority of 'thus sayeth the Lord'." [149]

4) GOVERNMENT SHOULD BE INVOLVED IN CHILD-REARING

Many have accepted the idea that government has authority over every area of life, including the family. Parents are no longer free to raise their children without

---

[148] John Hancock, in an "Oration on the Boston Massacre March 5, 1774", *The Magazine of History, with Notes and Queries*, Vol. 24, No. 95 (1923), pp 125, 136.

[149] House, H. W. (1999). *Christian Ministries and the Law: Revised edition* (38–39). Grand Rapids, Mich.: Kregel.

government interference. Every day, government agents intrude into the homes of law-abiding people to take their children away by force with nothing more than an unsubstantiated allegation of abuse. Children are being taken away from their parents simply because they used corporal punishment to discipline their children.

Are Christians not aware of the fact that use of "the rod" or paddle is not only promoted by the Bible in **Prov.13:24**, **19:18**, **22:15**, **23:13-14**, **29:15**, but it has been an accepted and effective form of disciplining children for millenniums? When done properly with firmness and love, it humbles the recalcitrant child rather than harms him.

The disciplinary mandates of the Bible are for the good of a child who needs correction. To allow a child to continue on a defiant, self-destructive course without receiving punishment in order to teach him humility is unwise and unloving.

> *He who withholds his rod hates his son, but he who loves him disciplines him diligently.* **Proverbs 13:24**

Must parents give up their liberty and stop disciplining their children because the state forbids it? Do children belong to their parents or to the state? Should parents disobey God in order to comply with a godless government?

Only evil governments and evil organizations take children away from their parents for complying with biblical child-rearing principles. Any judge who approves or participates in such an atrocity should be impeached and/or imprisoned.

If there is substantial proof that parents have abused their children, then the government has the responsibility of dealing with them in order to protect the children. But we must not forget that God has designated parents to be the authority over their children, not the state, Child Protective Services, or local school boards.

It does not take a village to rear a child!

The courts seem to be on the side of government intrusion in this matter, but God is on the side of parents. It remains to be seen whether the people will have the resolve to keep the government out of their personal lives.

5) LOYALTY TO COUNTRY REQUIRES SUBMISSION TO GOVERNMENT

We have discussed this and how so many associate loyalty to country with submission to government, but they are not the same. Sometimes, loyalty to country requires resistance to government. When government officials forget that they are our servants and start acting like our masters, we are forced to decide where to place our loyalty: to government, or to liberty.

The following are excerpts from an article from Pastor Chuck Baldwin entitled, "My Country, Right or Wrong", May 4, 2010:

> "To America's founders, patriotism had everything to do with the love of liberty, not the love of government! Today's brand of patriotism (at least as expressed by many) is totally foreign to the fundamental principles of liberty upon which America was built. I'm talking about the idea that government is an end and aim in itself; the idea that government must be protected from the people; the idea that bigger government equals better government; the idea that criticism of the government makes one

unpatriotic; the idea that government is a panacea for all our ills; and the idea that loyalty to the nation equals loyalty to the government. All of this is a bunch of bull manure!"

"When government - ANY GOVERNMENT - stops protecting the liberties of its citizens, and especially when it begins trampling those liberties, it has become a destructive power, and needs to be altered or abolished. Period!

"Can any honest, objective citizen not readily recognize that the current central government in Washington, D.C., long ago stopped protecting the God-given rights of free men and has become a usurper of those rights? Is there the slightest doubt in the heart of any lover of liberty that the biggest threat to our liberties is not to be found in any foreign capital, but in that putrid province by the Potomac?

"Therefore, we must cast off this phony idea that we owe some kind of devotion to the 'system'. Away with the notion that vowing to protect and prolong the 'powers that be' makes us 'good' Americans. The truth is, there is very little in Washington, D.C., that is worthy of protecting or prolonging. The 'system' is a ravenous BEAST that is gorging itself on our liberties!

"...Patriotism means we love freedom. It means we understand that freedom is a gift of God. It means we understand that government has only one legitimate function: to protect freedom. It means that our love of liberty demands that we oppose, alter, or even abolish ANY FORM of government that becomes destructive to these ends. And it means that we will never allow government to steal liberty from our hearts."

We don't have to tolerate a government when it is no longer "a minister of God for good". God gives us the right to defend ourselves against criminals on the street and the same applies to criminals in office who have much more power to harm us.

> "My own line of reasoning is to myself as straight and clear as a ray of light. Not all the treasures of the world, so far as I believe, could have induced me to support an offensive war, for I think it murder; but if a thief breaks into my house, burns and destroys my property, and kills or threatens to kill me, or those that are in it, and to bind me in all cases whatsoever to his absolute will, am I to suffer it? What signifies it to me, [I don't care] whether he who does it is a king or a common man; my countryman or not my countryman; whether it be done by an individual villain, or an army of them? If we reason to the root of things we shall find no difference; neither can any just cause be assigned why we should punish in the one case and pardon in the other." [150]

We can surely identify with the prophet Habakkuk:

> *...Yes, destruction and violence are before me; strife exists and contention arises. 4) Therefore the law [natural law] is ignored and justice is never upheld. For the wicked surround the righteous; therefore, justice comes out perverted.* **Habakkuk 1:3-4**

Those who are loyal to God will also be loyal to liberty, which means that they will be disloyal to oppressive government. We must abandon the false notion that love of country requires acceptance and submission to repressive laws and dictatorial leaders. We should love our country because it protects our rights to be free and independent people.

---

[150] Thomas Paine, *The Crisis,* Dec. 23, 1776.

CHAPTER 9

OPTIONS FOR KEEPING OUR FREEDOM

If possible, so far as it depends on you, be at peace with all men. **Romans 12:18**

MEEKNESS IF POSSIBLE

Christians should try to get along with people, but they are not required to be pacifists or to avoid controversy at any cost. We all know that it is impossible to always be at peace with all men.

"Many religious persons have a dread of controversy and wish truth to be stated without any reference to those who hold opposite errors. Controversy and a bad spirit are, in their estimation, synonymous terms. And to strenuously oppose what is wrong is considered as contrary to Christian meekness. Those who hold this opinion seem to overlook what every page of the New Testament lays before us. In all the history of our Lord Jesus Christ, we never find Him out of controversy. From the moment He entered on the discharge of His office in the synagogue in Nazareth till He expired on the cross, it was an uninterrupted scene of controversy. Nor did He, with all the heavenly meekness which in Him shone so brightly, treat truth and error without reference to those who held them... His censures were not confined to doctrine but included the abettors of false principles themselves. There is a loud call on all Christians to...present a firm and unified phalanx of opposition to error under every name – from whatever quarter it may approach." [151]

REFUSE TO TURN THE OTHER CHEEK

But I say to you, do not resist an evil person; but whoever slaps you on your right cheek, turn the other to him also. **Matthew 5:39**

Some take the command to "turn the other cheek" beyond the context in which it was given.

> "The verb 'resist' in verse 39 means to set oneself against or to oppose a person or a power. Not to resist here is the opposite of 'an eye for an eye', the lex talionis or law of retaliation found in the Mosaic Law. The law appears in contexts of civil code for theocratic national Israel. But Jesus is not speaking in a civil context to governing officials in Matthew 5, but to his individual disciples about their personal behavior. Rather than use the lex talionis as a pretext for exacting personal revenge (what the Jews had apparently done with this law), Jesus' followers are not to retaliate at all." [152]

Jesus was not commanding Christians to be pacifists.

> "He [Jesus] was not teaching unlimited nonresistance, but rather that the believer must have the spirit of nonresistance so that he retaliates only as a last resort, and then in the continued spirit of love. The command does not mean that Christians may never

---

[151] Robert Haldane, *"Fear of Controversy"*, 1874.

[152] Gardoski, K. "Jesus and War". In *Vol. 14: Journal of Ministry and Theology* (2010). (1) (16–17). Clarks Summit, PA: Baptist Bible College.

defend themselves. The point is that they should refrain from revengeful retaliation." [153]

On a personal level, we are to tolerate a measure of bad behavior without retaliation. If someone insults us by slapping us in the face, we are not to react in the same way as when a criminal violently attacks us. The purpose of a slap is to insult, not to harm or to cause injury. <u>We tolerate a slap but not criminal violence</u>. If someone attacks us or abuses us, we have every right to defend ourselves.

> "If our life be in danger from plots, or from open violence, or from the weapons of robbers or enemies, every means of securing our safety is honorable. For laws are silent when arms are raised...." [154]

The Lord specifically designated the right cheek that received the slap (Matt. 5:39). This demonstrates that the slap was *an insult* to be tolerated and not *an attack* which is not to be tolerated. In the first century, most people were right-handed just as they are today. They normally strike with the right hand when trying to hurt someone which would cause injury on the left cheek of someone facing them. Jesus' designation of the right cheek indicates that He was referring to a backhanded slap which is often used to insult a person but not to harm them. It is tempting for some to lift the phrase, "do not resist an evil person" out of context.

---

[153] David L. Plaster, "The Christian and War: A Matter of Personal Conscience", Vol. 6: *Grace Theological Journal.1985* (447). Winona, IN: Grace Seminary.

[154] Marcus Tullius Cicero, *Orations of Marcus Tullius Cicero*, Colonial Press, (1900), 204.

They take what is obviously referring to *personal issues* between family and friends and try to apply it to *civil issues* between citizens and government. They do the same thing with the phrase "Do not repay evil for evil" which is found in Rom. 12:17, 1 Thes. 5:15, and 1 Pet. 3:9. All of these Scriptures pertain to personal relationship issues, not civil issues concerning government. The Apostle Peter describes proper behavior between Christians in the verse below.

> *"Finally, all of you, have unity of mind, sympathy, brotherly love, a tender heart, and a humble mind. 9) Do not repay evil for evil or reviling for reviling, but on the contrary, bless, for to this you were called, that you may obtain a blessing."* **1 Peter 3:8-9**

The command, "Do not repay evil for evil" is another way of saying, "Two wrongs don't make a right." It is wrong for a Christian to retaliate when he is slapped or insulted, he is not to seek revenge but to put the matter in the Lord's hands. This has nothing to do with citizens resisting governmental abuse.

When Jesus called the Pharisees "vipers" and threw the money-changers out of the Temple for their evil actions, was He repaying evil for evil? No, He was taking a stand for righteousness. He resisted evil rulers who were oppressing the people. His actions show that verbal accusations and physical force are sometimes necessary to stand for righteousness and to protect others.

People in nations that have been occupied by invaders sometimes find it necessary to turn the other cheek to their occupiers by tolerating their evil until they have enough power to resist them.

"It is only in a period of civil impotence that Christians are under the rule to 'resist not evil'." [155]

When the de facto authority weakens, the ethic of "turning the other cheek" no long applies. This principle could explain why the Jews did not actively resist Rome during the time of Christ. Later, when they were stronger, they aggressively resisted their Roman occupiers.

VOTING THE SCOUNDRELS OUT OF OFFICE

Many believe the solution to getting our freedoms back is to simply vote the scoundrels out of office. That sounds simple enough, but if it's that easy, why hasn't it worked? The scoundrels are still there. We have voted and voted and voted and still languish under the heavy hand of a bloated and domineering government.

One problem is that possibly ninety-five percent of the candidates running for office have little or no character or integrity. I will be blunt. The majority of them are a pack of arrogant, vacillating, self-serving liars. Since people cannot find candidates they can truly support, they vote for candidates who are the lesser of two evils. What do you get when you vote for the lesser of two evils? That's right. Evil.

People who vote for a third party candidate or one that the media claims has no chance of winning are often accused of throwing their vote away. Ralph Boryszewski, a former policeman in New York City, has a great response for people who make such a claim:

---

[155] John M. Frame's "The Institutes of Biblical Law", article in *Westminster Theological Journal,* Volume 38. 1975 (2) (196).

"For years I have been voting for and supporting minor party candidates. People ask why do I always pick a loser and waste my vote. I make those poor souls think twice when I tell them: 'No I am picking a winner who will lose. But you, my friends, have been picking losers who always win.'" [156]

Voting makes people feel good about themselves because it makes them feel like they have done their civic duty, but voting does not result in better government when the entire field of candidates is unworthy of the people's trust or of holding office.

Many people vote, not because they are enthusiastic about any particular candidate, but because they don't want anyone to think ill of them for not voting. It's true that some people don't vote because they don't care about who governs them, but many do not vote because there is no candidate worthy of their support.

Most candidates will do or say anything in order to get elected, but once they take office, most, if not all of their pledges and promises are forgotten. So voting for what appears to be a good candidate does not mean he or she will be a good public servant once in office.

Honesty, virtue, and integrity in political candidates do not seem to be characteristics that are important to voters anymore. Very few candidates tell the truth. The majority of them are prevaricators and deceivers who make pledges they have no intention of keeping. They promise to give voters what they want, all the while knowing they will violate their oath to the Constitution in order to deliver such phony-baloney promises.

---

[156] Ralph Boryszewski, *The Constitution That Never Was*, 1995, xviii.

It seems like the shrewdest, most slick-talking candidates who sling the most mud to besmirch their opponents are the ones most likely to win elections.

And then, some voters cling to the notion that our problems can be solved by a particular political party. These misguided souls vote on the basis of a candidate's political affiliation rather than his character, record, or views on the issues.

> "Do we have a two party system in America today? I think not. We have one Big Government Party. It has a Republican wing that prefers war, deficits, assaults on civil liberties, and corporate welfare; and a Democratic wing that prefers war, taxes, assaults on commercial liberties, and individual welfare. Neither wing is devoted to the Constitution, and members of both wings openly mock it." [157]

Voting is a sacred right, but we must face the facts: It hasn't provided the changes we have hoped for. If it had, we wouldn't be in the mess we're in today.

> "For decades, we've been trading Democrats for Republicans, Republicans for Democrats, liberals for conservatives, and conservatives for liberals, and nothing has changed--except the problems keep getting worse!" [158]

The gullibility and lack of discernment of the typical American voter is nearly unbelievable. They keep voting the same forked-tongue crooks back into office over and over again. The Bible warns against such naiveté:

---

[157] Judge Andrew P. Napolitano, *It Is Dangerous To Be Right When the Government Is Wrong*. p. 263.

[158] Chuck Baldwin, "The Fear of God Is Not in This Place", Archived Column, July 19, 2012.

This is my warning to my people", says the LORD Almighty. "Do not listen to these prophets [politicians] *when they prophesy* [make promises] *to you, filling you with futile hopes. They are making up everything they say. They do not speak for the LORD!"* **Jeremiah 23:16**

Here is the biblical model for choosing leaders:

Furthermore, you shall select out of all the people <u>able men who fear God</u>, men of truth, those who hate dishonest gain; and you shall place these over them, as leaders of thousands, of hundreds, of fifties and of tens. **Exodus 18:21**

How many politicians running for office today fear (respect) God? How many are men and women of truth who hate dishonest gain? How many honor their word?

"All of our political and military leaders pay lip service to this 'rule of law', and all of them solemnly swear to uphold, obey, and defend the Constitution. However, for many of them, in this area as in so many others, their oaths of office are meaningless, empty words that they regularly ignore and willingly violate." [159]

Sadly, there are voters who only care about which candidate is more likely to give them the biggest piece of the government welfare pie.

And with the ongoing exposure of serious voter fraud, many wonder how legitimate the elections really are. Some say that it's not the number of votes cast but the number of votes counted that determines who wins elections.

---

[159] George B. Wallace, "Proper Use of the U.S. Military", *The New American Magazine,* July 5, 2010, p.12.

There is also the issue of ineligible voters who cast votes. We know that Illegal aliens vote and there are people who vote using the names of deceased people. How vigilant has our government been to protect the integrity of our election process? It has been reported that votes are already programmed in some voting machines before anyone casts a single vote.

> "Despite many instances of electoral fraud internationally, in the U.S. a major study by the Justice Department between 2002 and 2007 showed of the 300 million votes cast in that period, federal prosecutors convicted only 86 people for voter fraud, and of those few cases, most involved persons who were simply unaware of their ineligibility."[160]

With less than desirable candidates to choose from and so many voters being uninformed about candidates and issues, many are coming to the conclusion that the system is so disconnected, dysfunctional, corrupted by politicians and fraught with fraud that it is irreparable.

CONSTITUTIONAL GRAND JURIES & TRIAL JURIES

Our founders provided a way for us to safeguard freedom and preserve justice through our jury system. Americans actually operate under a three vote system:

1st Vote at the polls on election day
2nd Vote as a juror on a Grand Jury
3rd Vote as a juror on a Trial Jury

The vote of grand jurors and trial jurors was designed to be the last line of defense against tyranny.

---

[160] *Rolling Stone Magazine*, "The GOP War on Voting", retrieved 4-7-2012, *http://en.wikipedia.org/wiki/Voting_fraud*.

A person arrested for a capital crime cannot even be tried in court until he has been indicted by a Grand Jury of his peers who have determined that there is sufficient evidence to merit a trial (Article 5 of the Bill of Rights).

> "When someone is acting as a jury member during a courtroom trial, he has more power than the President, all of Congress, and all of the Judges combined. Congress can legislate (make law), the President or some other bureaucrat can make an order or issue regulations, and judges may instruct or make decisions, but no juror can ever be punished for voting 'Not Guilty!' A juror can, with impunity, choose to disregard the instructions of any judge or attorney in rendering his vote. If only one juror should vote 'Not Guilty' for any reason, there is no conviction and no punishment at the end of the trial. Thus, those acting in the name of government must come before the common man to get permission to enforce law." [161]

So, the principle that submission to our conscience supersedes submission to unjust laws was born out in our system of law consisting of independent jurors on Grand Juries and Trial Juries. Contrary to what many judges tell juries these days, every juror has the right to judge not only the facts of the case, but also the law.

Today, most jurors are unaware of this freedom so they feel obligated to comply with the misinformation given them by judges. They are afraid to vote their conscience when someone is charged with violating a law that they consider to be unjust. Until jurors acquire the knowledge and courage to judge both the law and

---

[161] *Citizens Rule Book, Jury Handbook,* p. 4.

the facts in their deliberations, innocent people will continue to be fined and incarcerated unjustly.

> "But juries are frequently influenced by the opinions of judges. They are sometimes induced to find special verdicts, which refer the main question to the decision of the court. Who would be willing to stake his life and his estate upon the verdict of a jury acting under the auspices of judges who had predetermined his guilt?" [162]

If a person is guilty of breaking a color of law code, rule, regulation or statute, but the juror considers the law to be oppressive or an encroachment on his freedom, he has the right to declare that person "innocent". This is the last judicial resort we have to protect ourselves from unjust laws and corrupt officials.

> "The pages of history shine on the instances of the jury's exercise of its prerogative to disregard instructions of the judge..." *U.S. vs. Dougherty,* 473 F 2nd 1113, 1139, (1972)

> "The jury has the right to judge the law as well as the fact in controversy." John Jay, 1st Chief Justice U.S. Supreme Court, 1789

> "The law itself is on trial quite as much as the cause which is to be decided." Harlan F. Stone, 12th Chief Justice U.S. Supreme Court, 1941

> "The jury has the right to determine both the law and the facts. "Samuel Chase, U.S. Supreme Court Justice, 1796, Signer of the unanimous Declaration

These Supreme Court decisions may be surprising to some but they shouldn't be. An act that is inherently

---

[162] Alexander Hamilton, *Federalist Papers # 65 (1787).*

immoral or unjust does not turn into a moral or just act simply because it is called a "law". *The government and the courts do many things that are legal, but that does not make them right, just, or lawful.*

> "Legality alone is no decent guide for a moral people. There are many things in this world that have been, or are, legal but clearly immoral. Slavery ... Nazi persecution of Jews, Stalin's and Mao's purges were all legal but did that make them moral?" [163]

We are all subject to Natural Law which is the law *"written in our hearts",* Rom. 2:15. William Blackstone, a devoted Christian scholar, once again worded it so well:

> "This law of nature, being coeval [having the same age or duration] with mankind and dictated by God himself, is of course superior in obligation to any other. It is binding over all the globe, in all countries, and at all times: no human laws are of any validity, if contrary to this; and such of them as are valid derive all their force, and all their authority, mediately or immediately, from this original." [164]

Citizens Rule Book... A Jury Handbook

This is a pocketsize booklet everyone should own that can be purchased on ebay.com or amazon.com for a few dollars. It contains The Bill Of Rights, The Declaration of Independence, and The Constitution for the United States. It includes a small compilation of quotes from founders and is a great help, not only for jurors, but for any American who wants to be free.

---

[163] Brian Farmer, "Is Soaking the Rich the Right Answer?" *The New American*, March 4, 2013, p. 19.

[164] Source: William Blackstone, *Of The Nature of Laws in General.*

INTERPOSITION IS PREFERABLE

Interposition is also known as the doctrine of lesser magistrates. It refers to a lesser authority standing between an abusive higher authority and those being abused. An example of this in our country would be state congressmen and/or governors, or local sheriffs opposing an unjust or unconstitutional action of the federal government that has been forced upon the people.

> "The legal interposition of one governmental level between a higher level of government and the people can thus lead to nullification of an act of tyranny, which is defined as the application of lawful force. In a self-governing republic like the United States of America, tyranny is equivalent to the arrogation of unconstitutional powers by the ruling authorities at any level of government." [165]

It is the responsibility of lesser government officials to obey their oath to the Constitution and to protect the people by refusing to carry out unjust mandates from higher officials.

When should lower governing officials interpose themselves between higher governing, evil officials and the people?

1. When they openly impugn the Law or Word of God.
2. When they attack the person, property, or freedom of someone in their jurisdiction.
3. When they try to enforce laws that are unconstitutional.

---

[165] Tom Rose, "Reconstruction and the American Republic", *Christianity and Civilization*, Geneva Divinity School Press, 1983, p. 297.

"Citing Romans chapter 13, Rev. West pointed out that civil magistrates are 'ministers of God' and therefore draw their authority from God's law. He resounded that when the civil magistrate subverts the authority given by God it is the duty of lesser magistrates to resist them." [166]

It has been slow in coming, but there are promising signs that state officials are beginning to protect their people from the federal government's unfunded and unconstitutional mandates. They are asserting their Constitutional Tenth Amendment right by passing laws that will nullify the overreach coming out of Washington D.C.

"A Rasmussen poll released Monday indicates that nullification is growing more and more popular in mainstream America. Pollsters found 38 percent support states taking actions to 'block' federal acts that restrict the right to keep and bear arms... 52 percent of mainstream voters think states should have the right to block any federal laws they disagree with on legal grounds." [167]

Anyone within the chain of command can and should abide by his oath of office to protect the people from anyone or anything that would encroach on their freedoms or rights.

"Is there not in these Untied States of America even one State Assembly, not even one board of county commissioners, not even one city council who will interpose themselves, as did the elders of ancient Israel with Rehoboam, between the growing tyranny

---

[166] Randy Pope, *http://lwhf.com/black_regiment.html*.

[167] Mike Maharrey, "Rasmussen Poll: Nullification Goes Mainstream", *Tenth Amendment Center, May*-6-2013.

of our national government and the long-suffering, overtaxed American people? This route of government interposition should still be tried before Americans individually 'go to their tents' in tax rebellion." [168]

When King Rehoboam made it clear that he intended to treat those in his kingdom harshly, there were elders who counseled him not to go through with his intentions. They put themselves between the king and the people to prevent him from oppressing them, 1 Kings 12:7.

Several sheriffs have committed themselves to keeping federal agents out of their counties who are intent on carrying out unconstitutional acts on the people.

Sheriff Richard Mac from Arizona is well-known for winning a suit against the Clinton administration in 1994 in a Tenth Amendment case that went all the way to the Supreme Court. He authored several books and formed The Constitutional Sheriffs and Peace Officers Association in order to encourage law enforcement officers to obey their oaths to the Constitution and to protect the rights of the people.

He also formed the County Sheriff Project of America where sheriffs from across the nation meet annually to demonstrate that state sovereignty coupled with local autonomy can produce solutions to our problems.

Sheriff Nick Finch was the patriotic hero who interposed himself between the State of Florida and an innocent man who was arrested for carrying a gun without a permit. Details are given later on page 221.

---

[168] Tom Rose, "Reconstruction and the American Republic", *Christianity and Civilization,* Geneva Divinity School Press, 1983, p. 295.

Author and radio talk show host, Mark Lavin, has just completed a book called *The Liberty Amendments* that promotes a form of interposition. It highlights article 5 of the U.S. Constitution which can be used as a form of interposition. It allows the people to rein in a federal government that is out of control by bypassing the President and Congress and calling for state conventions to propose amendments to the Constitution that would become law upon ratification by three fourths of the several states.

NULLIFICATION OR SECESSION

Millions of Americans would be appalled if someone suggested that certain states or groups of people should break away from the tyranny of our federal government to form a new union with a new government that respected their rights. But is it more important to preserve a political institution that is out of control or preserve the liberty which that political institution is supposed to secure?

Our founding fathers and the Colonists who separated from England certainly knew the answer to that question. The freedom-loving people of Maine, Vermont, Kentucky, and West Virginia knew it also. They seceded from existing U.S. states to create free and independent states.

> "Many great minds in this country are already philosophizing over the possibility that secession is an idea whose time has come--again. A few years ago, Walter Williams wrote, 'Like a marriage that has gone bad, I believe there are enough irreconcilable differences between those who want to control and those want to be left alone that divorce is the only peaceable alternative. Just as in a marriage, where

vows are broken, our human rights protections guaranteed by the U.S. Constitution have been grossly violated by a government instituted to protect them. Americans who are responsible for and support constitutional abrogation have no intention of mending their ways. Americans who wish to live free have two options: We can resist, fight and risk bloodshed to force America's tyrants to respect our liberties and human rights, or we can seek a peaceful resolution of our irreconcilable differences by separating.'" [169]

"What difference does it make if we have a 50-State Union or not? There is a bill in the California legislature that would divide that State into six states. Five counties in Western Maryland are trying to secede from Baltimore. Ten northern counties in Colorado are trying to secede from Denver. If a State refuses to secure the liberties of the people of that State, they have every right under God to separate. The State is not nearly as important as the liberties of the people within the State." [170]

"As an institution, the U.S. federal government is apostate. Yet, millions of citizens continue to make excuses for it, justify it, and condone it. They are more interested in preserving the agencies and entities and power of the institution. Yet, all the while, they are being enslaved by the very institution they are helping to prop up. What happens when an institution becomes more important than the cause for which the institution was formed? When the institution is civil government and the cause is liberty, tyranny is what happens." [171]

---

[169] Chuck Baldwin, *Institutionalized Tyranny*, March 27, 20014
[170] *Ibid*
[171] *Ibid*

CHAPTER 10

RESISTANCE WHEN NECESSARY

DID JESUS RESIST?

Some say that since Jesus never resisted governing authorities, neither should we. But is it true that he never resisted? The scribes and Pharisees [lawyers] were the governing authorities directly over the Jews, and on several occasions, Jesus resisted their efforts to control Him.

> *Then some Pharisees and scribes came to Jesus from Jerusalem, saying, 2) "Why do Your disciples transgress the tradition of the elders? For they do not wash their hands when they eat bread." 3) And He answered and said to them, "And why do you yourselves transgress the commandment of God for the sake of your tradition?"* **Matthew 15:1-3**

The Pharisees were alleging that Jesus' disciples were answerable to them for violating a tradition as if it was the law. Jesus fulfilled the Mosaic Law perfectly, but the issue they were confronting Him about was not part of that Law. The Pharisees were like so many politicians today: they went beyond their delegated authority and imposed traditions (codes, rules, and regulations) on people as if they were legitimate (Constitutional) laws.

Not only did Jesus refuse to instruct His disciples to submit to such pseudo laws, but He reprimanded the Pharisees for trying to turn traditions into laws and force them on others. He called them hypocrites and accused them of transgressing the commandment of God for the sake of their tradition.

One could argue that the hundreds of arbitrary statutes, codes, rules, and regulations being forced on us today that limit our freedoms could be compared to the traditions the Pharisees imposed on the Jews. Our prisons are overflowing with people who broke one of the countless government codes, statutes, or regulations but did no harm to others nor violated anyone's rights.

On another occasion, our Lord chided the Pharisees again for going beyond God's law to impose their own ideas and legalism on the people.

> *He* [Jesus] *was also saying to them* [scribes and Pharisees], *"You nicely set aside the commandment of God in order to keep your tradition* [in order to impose your own notions or regulations on the people]." **Mark 7:9**

Jesus' rebuke of them and His refusal to submit to the Pharisees' tradition demonstrate that an automatic, unconditional loyalty or submission to governing authorities is not required. Jesus did not require His disciples to submit to these Pharisees who were trying to enforce tradition/unconstitutional law, as if it were part of the Mosaic/constitutional law.

In Matthew 23, Jesus called the scribes and Pharisees who were the civil authority directly over the Jews "hypocrites", "blind guides", "fools", "whitewashed tombs full of dead men's bones", and "a brood of vipers".

> "Jesus Himself felt free to criticize not only the Jewish civil leaders, (John 18:23), but also the Roman-appointed ruler, Herod Antipas, in referring to

him as a 'fox' (Luke. 13:32). Jesus whipped the money changers and chased them out of the temple (John 2: 13-17). Following that, Christ would not allow any person to carry 'any vessel through the temple' (Mark. 11:16). Christ's act of whipping the money changers and blocking the entrance to the temple were crimes." [Ultimately Christ is portrayed in the Book of Revelation as exercising righteous vengeance on the secular humanistic state.] [172]

Holding court at night was against Jewish jurisprudence, so when the Pharisees were trying to gather evidence to execute Jesus during one of the seven unlawful trials, He refused to answer the High Priest's questions even though he insisted that Jesus answer him, Mark 14:60-61. He also refused to answer Pontius Pilate who was the Roman governor over Judea, Matt. 27:13-14.

Many try to portray Jesus as a weak, whimpering pacifist who avoided controversy and would never challenge the status quo. That certainly does not describe the Jesus Christ of the Bible. There was controversy over just about everything He said and did.

It is incorrect to say that we should submit to oppression without resistance because Jesus submitted to oppression. We must bear in mind that His life was unique and His death was unique. It was necessary for Him to suffer abuse in order to purchase the redemption of all mankind.

---

[172] John H. Whitehead, "Christian Resistance In the Face of State Interference", *Christianity and Civilization*, Geneva Divinity School, p. 7.

And according to Paul's custom, he went to them... 3) explaining and giving evidence that the Christ had to suffer and rise again from the dead. **Acts 17:2-3**

Some first century Christians were accused of acting contrary to the decrees of Caesar and were dragged before city authorities for allegedly turning the world upside down, Acts 17:6-7. But what was their crime? Acts 17:7 tells us:

"'*These all do contrary to the decrees of Caesar, saying that there is another king, one Jesus.* 'This was an act of political treason. A popular myth invoked by Christians and non-Christians alike to justify their refusal to stand against immoral acts of the State has been the assertion that Jesus and the apostles were pacifists. This is not true. The question of pacifism did not arise, but Jesus was certainly no quietist." [173]

The Apostle Peter and other apostles refused to obey governing authorities who commanded them to stop teaching the Word of God.

And when they had brought them, they stood them before the Council. And the high priest questioned them, 28) saying, "We gave you strict orders not to continue teaching in this name, and behold, you have filled Jerusalem with your teaching, and intend to bring this man's blood upon us." 29) But Peter and the apostles answered and said, "We must obey God rather than men." **Acts 5:27-29**

---

[173] John H. Whitehead, "Christian Resistance In the Face of State Interference", *Christianity and Civilization*, Geneva Divinity School, p. 7.

The Jews wanted to make Jesus king for their own purposes, mainly to deliver them from Roman occupation, John 6:15, 12:13. But He was on a mission to save mankind from their sins by bearing their punishment on the cross. He could not be distracted by getting embroiled in issues concerning the Roman occupation of Judea.

Any statement or action by Jesus against the Roman occupiers would have been a departure from His mission and would make it appear that deliverance from Rome was more important than delivering the world from sin. Christ came to free mankind from the penalty of sin, not to free the first century Christians from Roman occupation.

Alan Johnson wrote an article in the JETS Journal entitled, *"The Bible and War in America, A Social Survey"*, stating: "Still Reinhold Niebuhr could agree with the pacifist that Jesus taught nonresistance to evil, that human life ought not to be taken, and that the law of love is the law of life. Yet he concluded, against the pacifists, that this position of Jesus was not to be the Christian stance in terms of securing justice in a sinful world. The pure ethic of Jesus is not relevant to our real life situation; it must only have proximate value." [174]

There are several instances where Jesus escaped from the authorities that were trying to apprehend Him, John 7:30-32, 8:59, 10:39. If the Bible requires unconditional obedience to oppressive authority, He would have been obligated to turn himself in or allow

---

[174] Alan Johnson, "The Bible and War in America: An Historical Survey", *Journal of the Evangelical Theological Society.* Vol. 28: 1985 (2) (178–179). Lynchburg, VA: The Evangelical Theological Society.

them to apprehend Him. But He didn't do that. Instead, He resisted the civil authority's effort to apprehend Him.

The right to flee from abuse or to resist it is universal. Were it not so, innocent people, including women and children, would become fodder for merciless brutes who hold the reins of power.

EXAMPLES OF BIBLICAL CIVIL DISOBEDIENCE

When a Christian disobeys an unjust or immoral law, he is not showing contempt for legitimate authority or laws in general. He is actually demonstrating his respect for the **Rule of Law** and disdain for those who pervert it. Consider the following examples:

The Hebrew Midwives disobeyed a direct command from the king of Egypt and yet, God blessed them as well as the Hebrew people.

> *16) And he [Pharaoh] said, "When you [midwives] are helping the Hebrew women to give birth... if it is a son, then you shall put him to death...17) But the Hebrew midwives feared God, and did not do as the king of Egypt had commanded them but let the boys live... 20) So God was good to the midwives, and the people multiplied, and became very mighty.*
> ***Exodus 1:16-20***

Jochebed, the Mother of Moses also defied Pharaoh's command to execute her male child by hiding him and setting him afloat in a basket in the Nile River. God blessed her and all the Israelites because she refused to obey an immoral law. Exodus 2:1-3

Rahab, the Harlot was commanded by the king of Jericho to turn over the Hebrew men who were spying out the land and who visited her house, Joshua 2:1-18. She disobeyed and hid the men to avoid capture. God not only spared her life but the lives of her family as well. Everyone else in the city of Jericho was killed when the Israelites attacked. She is one of only four women mentioned in the Bible who are in the line of Jesus Christ, Matt. 1:5. She is also named in the list of heroes found in Hebrews 11:31.

King Saul's Elite Guards disobeyed his unlawful, direct order to kill the priests of the Lord in the city of Nob. God neither rebuked nor punished them,

> *And the king said to the guards who were attending him, "Turn around and put the priests of the LORD to death, because their hand also is with David and because they knew that he was fleeing and did not reveal it to me." But the servants of the king were not willing to put forth their hands to attack the priests of the Lord.* **1 Samuel 22:17**

Queen Esther ignored the law that forbade anyone from seeing the king without his permission in order to save herself and the Jewish people from a deadly plot. She broke the law in order to inform the king of the plot. It took great courage on her part because she could have been executed for defying the law. Through her heroic action, God spared her life and the lives of all the Jews, and the evil plotters were hung, Esther 5.

Shadrach, Meshach, and Abed-Nego disobeyed the order of King Nebuchadnezzar to bow down to a golden image in his likeness. The king threw them into an extremely hot furnace, but the Lord joined them in the fire and delivered them unharmed. They were willing to die rather than obey an unjust law, Daniel 3:1-30.

Daniel refused to obey a decree that King Darius made stating that anyone who prayed to any god or man besides himself for a period of thirty days would be thrown into the lions' den. The king had been manipulated by Daniel's jealous enemies to make the decree because they wanted to see him dead.

Daniel did not obey the decree and he prayed to God anyway. So he was thrown into the lion's den, yet he came out unharmed because God delivered him. Those who motivated the king to make the atrocious decree and who reported Daniel's disobedience were the ones thrown into the Lion's den along with their families, Daniel 6.

The Magi, who were trying to find Jesus, did not obey King Herod's command to report back to him when they had found Him. Had they obeyed the command, Herod would have tried to kill Jesus and probably the Magi as well. Yet God told them in a dream not to report back to Herod. They obeyed God rather than the king and their lives were spared, Matt. 2:1-12.

Joseph and Mary did not stick around and allow Jesus to be killed when King Herod ordered the death of Jewish male babies. God instructed them to flee to Egypt and He protected them on their journey. This is another illustration where God instructed His children to ignore unjust laws made by evil rulers, Matt. 2:13.

Peter and His Companions were commanded by Jewish religious leaders to stop preaching in Christ's name and were imprisoned for refusing to obey. They told their religious leaders who had authority over them:

We must obey God rather than men. **Acts 5:28-29**

God did not give man volition and then deny him the use of it by requiring unconditional submission to autocrats who possess de-facto power.

Moses: Did he violate God's principle of submission to authority when he went against Pharaoh's laws and killed an Egyptian taskmaster who was trying to beat a Hebrew slave to death? Exodus 2:11-12

Elijah: Did he violate God's principle of submission to authority when he publicly exposed and challenged the immoral and unjust activities of King Ahab and Queen Jezebel?

David: Did he violate God's principle of submission to authority when he refused to surrender to King Saul who was using state personnel and resources to hunt him down to murder him?

John the Baptist: Did he violate God's principle of submission to authority when he publicly scolded King Herod for his immoral acts? Mark 6: 17-20

The Apostle Peter: Did he violate God's principle of **submission** to authority when he refused to obey authorities who demanded that he abandon his missionary work? (Acts 5:29)

Our Lord Himself: Did He violate the principle of submission to authority when He evaded being arrested on several occasions by leaders of the Jewish establishment who were intent on killing Him?

Every Apostle of Christ experienced martyrdom from the hands of hostile civil authorities according to historians; the only exception being the Apostle John who escaped being boiled in oil. In addition, Christians throughout church history were imprisoned, tortured or killed by civil authorities for refusing to submit to their evil laws and prohibitions. Did any of these Christian martyrs violate God's principle of submission to authority? No.

"So even the great prophets, apostles, and writers of the Bible (including the writer of Romans chapter 13) understood that human authority, including civil authority, is limited." [175]

RESISTING TYRANNY IS NOT REVOLUTION

Do not be afraid of them; remember the Lord who is great and awesome, and fight for your brothers, your sons, your daughters, your wives and your houses.
Nehemiah 4:14

George Washington had a clear understanding of government. He said:

"Government is not reason; it is not eloquence; it is force! Like fire, it is a dangerous servant and a fearful master."

Hopefully, despotism can be thrown off without the use of arms, but despots don't usually relinquish their power without a fight.

"There may be circumstances in which revolution is the only alternative. If a government becomes so corrupt, so totally repressive, and so totally unjust as to destroy rather than promote the legitimate ends of government, revolution may then be justifiable either as a necessary good or as the lesser evil." [176]

---

[175] Chuck Baldwin, "Romans 13 Revisited", Feb.27, 2009, *NewsWithAView.Com*.

[176] John Eidsmoe, *God and Caesar, Biblical Faith and Political Action,* Wipf and Stock Publishers, p. 32.

It is suggested that the reference to "revolution" in the quote above means armed resistance as a last resort in defending oneself rather than meaning the violent overthrow of an existing government.

Having to use force to defend oneself against one's own government is a dreadful thought indeed. It is repugnant for most Americans to even consider such a thing. Most think it preposterous to believe that anything like that could possibly happen in "the land of the free".

That is what millions of people in other countries all over the world thought of their own homeland's, but they were wrong. The statistics of governments killing their own people over the past hundred years certainly confirm this.

Revolution involves *offensive aggression* against a government to overthrow it or to destroy it, whereas **Resisting Tyranny** is *defensive resistance* against abuse. God does not advocate nor condone revolution, but He does support efforts to maintain or reclaim freedom.

The "Revolutionary War" and the "Civil War" are not examples of revolution but are examples of legitimate resistance to tyranny. The term, "Revolutionary War", is a misnomer, meaning it is an incorrect or unsuitable name. It would be more accurate to refer to both of these as "Wars for Independence".

We know that the Colonists did not attack England nor did they try to overthrow King George whose oppression they could no longer abide. So they declared their independence and separated from him and England. When the king sent British soldiers to attack them, they had every right to defend themselves.

Both names, "The Civil War" and the "The War Between the States", are also misnomers because the Southern States did not try to topple the U.S. government nor did they try to overthrow the United States. They seceded from the Union and formed a new nation which the Declaration of Independence says is their right and duty. It was similar to what the colonies did when they separated from England eighty-five years earlier. The new nation was called "the Confederate States of America".

So it wasn't a "War Between the States" because the States that joined the Confederacy were no longer States of the Union.

Also, the Southerners were not rebels even though they were called rebels by northern leaders who were trying to generate support for the war. No, Southerners were not rebelling against the Union nor were they trying to reform, abolish, or overthrow it. They decided to secede because the North had no intention of respecting the Constitution of the United States or the sovereignty of the Southern States.

Congress continued to pass unreasonable laws that benefitted the North at the South's expense. President Lincoln did not accept the legitimacy of the Confederacy, so when he sent federal troops into the South, Southerners naturally defended their new nation which they had the right to do.

> "Revolution against authority is not the same as war against tyranny." [177]

> "Government is nothing more than an agent for God

---

[177] Pastor R.B. Thieme, Jr., *Laws of Divine Establishment,* page 2.

and for society. Consequently, there always remains a reserve of right in the people to remove their agent." [178]

These are weighty matters that should be very carefully considered. If Christians are not allowed to resist despotism, who will? Should that responsibility be solely imposed on unbelievers? Would that be pleasing to God: Christians standing on the sidelines while unbelievers risk everything to stand for freedom and justice?

Many today are confused about the relationship between Christians and their government. They have embraced the erroneous propaganda and notion that anyone who challenges the state is a rebel. Modern history books may promote that idea along with the media, but it is false. Our founding fathers were not wild, impulsive rebels; they were refined well-educated men. Many of them were Christians, thoroughly proficient in the Law and the Scriptures, who worked diligently to harmonize their actions with both.

> "Our founding fathers then, were not rebels or anarchists. They strongly believed in the divine institution of government, but they also believed that government must be founded on the law of God rather than the caprice of man." [179]

There is a continuing effort to remove every vestige of Christianity from our government as well as public and private life. But our nation was founded on the God of the Bible whose Son is the Lord Jesus Christ.

---

[178] Bodin, *On Sovereignty: Six Books on the Commonwealth*, p. 66.

[179] John Eidsmoe, *God and Caesar, Biblical Faith and Political Action,* Wipf and Stock Publishers, p. 35.

> "The faith of the founding fathers of this nation was in the God who is revealed in Christ. Many of the leaders of the war were Protestant clergy, theologians, and devoutly evangelical men, such as Samuel Adams and Patrick Henry." [180]

> "Our Colonial forefathers were astute students of the Bible, for they used God's holy word as their guide and rule in establishing every aspect of society; especially civil government, for they had suffered under the perversion of biblical teaching called 'the divine right of kings'." [181]

Those who founded our country were not only well-educated, they were also pragmatic because they knew that to try to maintain freedom without arms would be futile. That is why they knew they must stand against the British at Lexington and Concord or they would become slaves to King George. They enshrined the right to keep and bear arms for protection against criminals, in and out of office, in the 2nd Amendment to the Bill of Rights.

THE 2ND AMENDMENT: OUR ULTIMATE PROTECTION

> "A well-regulated militia, being necessary to the security of a free state, the right of the people to keep and bear arms, shall not be infringed."
> 2nd Amendment to the Bill of Rights

This amendment ultimately secures all of our other rights. It is not about the right to hunt, take target practice,

---

[180] House, H. W. *Christian Ministries and The Law:* Revised edition (25). Grand Rapids, Mich.: Kregel. (1999).

[181] Tom Rose, "Our Reconstruction and the American Republic", *Christianity and Civilization,* Geneva Divinity School Press, 1983, p. 287.

engage in sport shooting, or about being a gun collector. It's about having a last line of defense against an oppressive government that desires to enslave its own citizens. Because of this amendment, Americans can lawfully defend themselves with arms and keep tyrants from achieving their goals.

One of the first things Adolf Hitler did when he became Chancellor of Germany was to insist that people register their guns, which of course led to their confiscation. Any government officials who would pass a law limiting the God-given right for law-abiding citizens to defend themselves are either ignorant, which is doubtful, or planning something evil. They know criminals don't obey laws, so why pass gun laws they know will be ignored by criminals but will limit the ability of innocent people to defend themselves?

To suggest that we should not trust our own government because it is capable of becoming a police state or dictatorship can be upsetting to some. Yet who would deny that every government, including ours, is made up of men and women with inherent sinful natures and lust patterns which include the lust for money and power among other inordinate desires.

It is as natural for leaders to try to increase their power as it is for sparks to fly upwards, and if those leaders are not resisted, they will take over.

Lord Acton's famous axiom:

"Power tends to corrupt, and absolute power corrupts absolutely."

There have been reports that internment camps have been constructed in various places around our country. Most Americans don't believe it and think it's absurd to even suggest that innocent Americans could be rounded up by our government and forced to live in internment camps patrolled by armed guards.

They are unaware that it already happened here in 1942 when President Roosevelt issued an executive order that enabled our military to forcibly imprison innocent Japanese American citizens into internment camps.

These innocent Americans had their freedoms stripped away for one reason only; they were Japanese, the same race as those who bombed Pearl Harbor. They were forced to leave their homes and relocate to internment camps where there were curfews and no one could leave or enter without the permission of the military commander in charge. The Supreme Court upheld this executive order in *Korematsu v. United States* (1944).

> "What happens when a government ceases to be legitimate? When elected representatives disregard their Constitutional function, they cease being true representatives and therefore deserve to be resisted. For the sake and in the name of legitimate government, Rutherford believed Christians in that case are called to actively revolt." [182]

On November 10, 1798, The Kentucky Legislature declared:

> "Puritans were not content to let abject submission totally define their relationship with authority. Even more than persons living in a permissive society, they felt the need to raise defenses against the fathers

---

[182] House, H. W. (1999). *Christian Ministries and The Law,* Revised edition (26). Grand Rapids, Mich. p. 169-170.

who constantly threatened judgment and rebuke. The inward impulse was expressed in Puritan political philosophy as the doctrine of rights and the Rule of Law. Even conservatives asserted that 'God has not subjected the Lives and Liberties of the ruled, to the arbitrary will and pleasure of rulers.' He gave 'Laws to their authority', so that they were not 'at liberty to pursue and accomplish their own desire'. The law defined the line beyond which rulers became tyrants and resistance became a duty." [183]

GENOCIDE STATISTICS OVER THE PAST CENTURY
http://www.urbanministry.org/wiki/genocide-statistics

- Armenia from 1915-23: 1,000,000 killed
- China under Mao: 58,000,000 killed
- USSR under Stalin: 20,000,000 killed
  (Robert Conquest, The Great Terror)
- Holocaust from 1933-45: 5,700,000 killed
  (Nuremberg Trial)
- Khmer Rouge, Cambodia 1975-78: 1,600,000 killed
- Bosnia from 1992-95: 250,000 killed
  (U.S. State Dept.)
- Rwanda in 1994: 1,000,000 killed
- Somalia from 1991-present: 300,000 killed
  (IRIN, a UN agency)
- Darfur from 2003 to present: 450,000 killed
  (UN High Commission on Refugees)

TOTAL: Approximately <u>89 million people killed</u>

Other researchers have found the statistics to be even more shocking:

"Over the ages tyrants have ordered the complete annihilation of races and religions for no other reason than that the targeted groups didn't want to be ruled

---

[183] Richard L. Bushman, *From Puritan to Yankee: Character and the Social Order to Connecticut*, 1690-1765.

by the tyrants... University of Hawaii professor emeritus R.J. Rummel authored Statistics of Democide: Genocide and Mass Murder Since 1900. He gathered data that showed that over 170 million human beings were killed by their own governments during the 20th Century. Subsequent information gathered after the book was published revised the figure upward to a total of <u>262 million</u> – six times more people were killed by their own governments than died in all of the century's wars combined." [184]

These are very sobering statistics that should alert us to the inherent dangers associated with governments' inhumanity to man. Nearly all of these millions of people had one thing in common: *<u>they were unarmed</u>*. Our founding fathers knew how important an armed citizenry is when they included the 2nd Amendment as part of the Bill of Rights. ARMED CITIZENS ARE NOT EASILY ENSLAVED OR KILLED.

GUN CONTROL

Why are we allowing the State to fine or imprison law-abiding citizens for carrying a weapon without a permit? By what authority does it disarm people who have the God-given right to protect themselves and their families? What happened to the right to keep and bear arms? Isn't the 2nd Amendment still part of the Constitution? Isn't the Constitution still the supreme law of the land as stated in Article VI, Section 2? What's going on here?

If the politicians in Washington who actively push gun control could have their way, no one would possess guns except the military, the police, U.S. government

---

[184] Arthur R. Thompson, "War, War, War", *JBS Bulletin*, Mar'12, p. 2.

agents and United Nations "peace keepers". However, they face a couple of serious hurdles.

1. It is estimated that there are 300,000,000 guns in the United States (gunfaq.org).
2. The 2nd Amendment

These people are not stupid. They know that passing laws to make it illegal to own or carry a gun will have absolutely no effect on criminals, who, by definition, don't obey laws anyway. They have to know that their gun control laws only disarm law-abiding citizens and make it easier for criminals to prey on them. So what would motivate them to pass laws that put citizens in such danger?

They know that a well-armed citizenry can resist an overreaching government. They have tried to convince the public that guns are bad and are directly responsible for the horrific number of people murdered every year in our country.

However, guns are not bad. They are dangerous, as they must be in order to ward off criminals, and it is true that in a free society, there will be times when kooks will use guns to go on a shooting spree and murder innocent people. However, the solution to this problem is not to take guns away from law-abiding citizens. The solution is to encourage them to be armed so they are able to defend themselves and others.

Switzerland has one of the highest gun ownership rates in the world but ranks as low as 103 in its crime rate among the countries of the world.
(Source: *www.nationmaster.com/country-info/stats/Crime/Crime-levels*)

Advertising that our schools are gun-free zones invites mentally unstable and/or wicked monsters to prey on our children because such cowards go where they know the law prohibits guns.

It is also true that on rare occasions, innocent lives are lost when there are hunting accidents or when children accidently shoot another child, but it is the responsibility of parents to protect their children from such incidents and educate them in the use and misuse of guns.

What is not reported are the hundreds of thousands of innocent lives that are saved every year by people who defend themselves from criminals either by showing that they have a gun, or if necessary, using one. And fortunately, there are still brave patriots like this man:

A BRAVE CONSTITUTIONAL SHERIFF IN FLORIDA

Sheriff Nick Finch was charged by the State of Florida with felony "official misconduct" and "falsifying public records" after he had released a suspect who had been arrested on an unconstitutional gun charge. Sheriff Finch had also removed the suspect's arrest file.

> "During the trial, the sheriff testified that he released Floyd Eugene Parrish, who was arrested for unlawfully carrying a firearm, because *he believed the Second Amendment trumped all state gun laws*. As we reported back in June, the Florida Department of Law Enforcement accused Finch of covering up the arrest of Floyd Eugene Parrish after releasing him from the Liberty County Jail. On March 8, Sgt. James Joseph Hoagland of the Liberty County Sheriff's Office arrested Parrish during a traffic stop after finding a .25 automatic pistol in Parrish's right front pocket and a holstered revolver in his car, according to court records. Parrish was then taken to the county jail. After being notified of Parrish's arrest,

Finch took the arrest file and told jailers that Parrish would be released with no charges, according to investigators. Finch also ordered both the pistol and revolver to be returned." [Emphasis added] [185]

It took the jury less than 90 minutes to reach its verdict of "not guilty" and Sheriff Finch to resume his job of protecting the people in his county and of honoring and defending the Constitution.

Does the Bible also acknowledge the right of people to arm themselves against *anyone* who would harm them? Absolutely, and that includes all criminals, whether they are wearing a mask or a uniform.

> *When a strong man, fully armed, guards his own house, his possessions are undisturbed.* **Luke 11:21**

> *And He* [Jesus] *said to them* [His disciples], *"But now, whoever has a money belt is to take it along, likewise also a bag, and whoever has no sword is to sell his coat and buy one."* **Luke 22:36**

Our Lord demonstrated that it is more important to have a weapon for protection against criminals than it is to have a coat for protection against the cold. Of course there were no guns at that time, but if there were, He would have told His disciples to sell their coats and buy a gun.

When the British marched on Concord and Lexington to take away the arms and powder of the Colonists, Christians stood in front of their church and held their ground. Why? Because they knew that unarmed people become slaves.

---

[185] Alex Jones, "Pro-Gun Sheriff Found Not Guilty", *infowars.com*, Oct. 31, 2013.

Eight minutemen died on Lexington Green that day but their death was not in vain. It was the "shot that was heard around the world". The monument that honors those men states:

> "The blood of these martyrs, in the cause of God and their country, was the cement of the union of these states, the colonies."

Some would allege that these courageous Christian men were wrong to disobey the order of a British officer who commanded them to disperse since he represented established authority. But the fact that people do not forfeit their God-given rights when they become Christians has already been established. So they certainly had the right to protect themselves and their families from *anyone* who would take away their means of self-defense.

Why, as said before, would God allow us to resist evil in matters of faith but deny that same right in matters of freedom?

Every American soldier has the right and duty to protect our freedoms by resisting any evil force that threatens it. They take an oath to support and defend the Constitution of the United States of America against all enemies, foreign and domestic.

Why should only soldiers have that duty? Why should soldiers be granted that right but not the American people? If anyone, including those in Congress, judges on the Supreme Court, or the President, violates the rights of the people, they become domestic enemies that should be resisted.

The Declaration of Independence says:

"Whenever any form of government becomes destructive…it is the Right of the People to alter or abolish it." It also says, "…it is their right, it is their duty to throw off such a government, and to provide new Guards for their future security."

Unarmed people cannot defend themselves and are unable to throw off a tyrannical government. That is why our founders were wise enough to include the 2nd Amendment in the Bill of Rights which recognizes the right of the people to keep and bear arms.

JESUS' UNJUST ARREST

The account of Jesus' arrest found in all four gospels is very instructive regarding the right to resist evil. The Jewish High Priest and the Pharisees wanted to kill Jesus because they were jealous of His' growing popularity and were afraid that they were losing their legalistic control over the people. So they sent a detachment of at least two hundred Temple guards and Roman soldiers who were heavily armed with swords and clubs to apprehend Him because they were anticipating a fight.

Peter was determined to protect his Lord, so he drew his sword and cut off the ear of one of the soldiers in the advancing mob. Then Jesus ordered Peter:

> *"Put your sword back into its place, for all those who take up the sword shall perish by the sword."*
> **Matt. 26:52**.

Most people think Jesus was rebuking Peter for committing a crime when he resisted the henchmen who were sent to make the arrest. However, another way of looking at it is that the rebuke was not directed toward Peter at all but toward the soldiers, Temple guards, and the evil leaders who had sent them. Let's look at the facts:

1. Jewish leaders sent soldiers and guards out in the middle of the night to arrest an innocent man without a warrant in order to have Him stand trial that very night. In doing so, they were breaking not only God's natural laws but their own laws as well. Night trials were illegal as were nighttime arrests.

   "The provisions relating to criminal trials, and especially to those in which the offense was punishable by death, were very stringent and were all framed in the interest of the accused. Among them were the following: The trial must be begun by day, and if not completed before night it must be adjourned and resumed by day;" [186]

2. They were in a hurry to have Him killed so they could celebrate the Passover in peace.

   "Roman soldiers [were] subject to the ordinary law applicable to everyone else... Roman law's rule [provided] that at night it is as permissible to oppose a soldier who is breaking in, just as you would resist any other person, since no respect needs to be shown a soldier who has to be opposed with a weapon, as if he were a robber." [187]

3. Jesus indicated his arrest was unjust when He told His disciples:

   "See, the hour is at hand, and the Son of Man is betrayed into the hands of sinners." **Matt. 26:45**

---

[186] Heading II. *The Jewish Trial,* Point #3:
http://bibleencyclopedia.com/arrest.htm

[187] David B. Kopel, *The Torah and Self-Defense,* p. 70.

4. When the disciples recognized what was happening, they asked Jesus, *"Lord, shall we strike with the sword?" Luke 22:49*. The Bible does not record whether Jesus responded to their question, but it does record Peter using his sword to defend Christ, Luke 22:50. It is possible that Peter didn't wait for a response before he struck, or maybe he took Jesus' silence as an affirmation that he could strike.

5. Peter did not strike with his sword until after the mob laid hands on Jesus and seized Him, Matt. 26:50-51. It is possible that the mob seized Jesus immediately after the disciples' query about striking with the sword but before He could respond, so Peter did not hesitate to defend his Lord.

6. *Jesus said, "Permit even this." (KJV) Luke 22:51*. He was explaining to Peter that His unlawful arrest was a necessary part of God's plan for Him to go to the cross so Peter needed to stop resisting the soldiers.

7. Jesus also explained to Peter that twelve legions of angels were at His disposal had they been needed to resist the soldiers and their evil superiors, Matt. 26:53. Jesus would never have said that if resisting injustice was wrong.

8. Peter's timing was off; he did the right thing but it was at the wrong time. Jesus pointed out to Peter that this unjust arrest had to take place in order to fulfill the Scriptures, Matt. 26:56.

9. Jesus did not scold Peter for having a military sword even though it was against Roman law for Jews to possess one.

> "Under Roman law, citizens had a right to carry personal arms... [However], Roman law forbade Jews and other subject people to carry swords under penalty of death. Apparently, the apostles of Jesus violated the law by carrying a pair of swords." [188]

10. Furthermore, Jesus did not order Peter to give up his sword but to simply put it back into its scabbard, Matt. 26:52.

11. Jesus did not reprimand Peter because Peter was obeying the Scriptures that required Jews to defend the innocent. (NET) Lev.19:16, teaches that you must not stand idly by when your neighbor's life is in jeopardy.

12. But in the eyes of the soldiers and their corrupt leaders, Peter had committed a capital crime. Even so, the soldiers did not touch him because Jesus would not permit it, John 18:8-9.

13. Since Jesus is perfectly righteous, He would never protect someone who was guilty of a serious crime from being punished. As deity, He cannot show partiality, and if Peter were guilty, Jesus would have been obligated to turn him over to the soldiers to be punished or executed.

14. There is no way that Jesus would be just in taking the side of evil men who were breaking the law by oppressing someone innocent. By doing so, He would be condoning persecution and condemning self-defense.

15. Jesus rebuked the Temple guards for treating Him as if he were a violent criminal when they knew otherwise, Matt. 26:56.

---

[188] David B. Kopel, *The Human Right Of Self-Defense,* pg. 111.

16. The logical conclusion is found in what Jesus told Peter: **"Those who live by the sword"** live by violence, **"will die by the sword"** in that they will receive just punishment. He was not referring to Peter but to the armed wicked men who were carrying out an evil plot against an innocent man!

17. Jesus' statements to Peter were said to reassure him and the other disciples that anyone who commits sinful acts against the innocent will receive just punishment for their shameful crimes. This would motivate Peter and the other disciples to back off which would defuse the situation so that the arrest could be carried out and Jesus would make it to the cross.

God warned kings who fell into evil and multiplied their transgressions to heed His warnings or they would "die by the sword", Job 36:7-12. God promised that evil thrones and kingdoms would "die by the sword", Haggai 2:2. Samaria "fell by the sword" because she rebelled against the Lord, Hosea 13:6.

In Revelation 13:10, God encourages believers who will be in the Tribulation with information that the anti-Christ and his minions will be dealt with by Him, personally. Any effort by believers to resist him will be futile, but God assures them that he [anti-Christ] who leads people into captivity and kills them with the sword will be "killed with the sword". This will encourage saints in the Tribulation to avoid confrontation because they know that Jesus Christ Himself will destroy their oppressors.

"He [anti-Christ] who leads into captivity shall go into captivity; he [anti-Christ] who kills with the sword

*must be killed with the sword. Here is the patience and the faith of the saints." **Rev. 13:10** (KJV)*

Jesus told Pilate, "My kingdom is not of this world. If My kingdom were of this world, then My servants would be fighting so that I would not be handed over to the Jews; but as it is, My kingdom is not of this realm. ***John 18:36***

Jesus was assuring Pilate that he need not be concerned that He might be a revolutionary intending to overthrow Rome. However, He did affirm the right to resist oppression when he pointed out that if His kingdom were of this world, His servants would be fighting against injustice.

MEN OF RENOWN RESISTED TYRANNY

For a long time, men have recognized the limitations of government and the right of common men to defend themselves against abuse that occurs when those limitations are ignored. Many renowned men have spoken out over the years on the right to resist tyranny. The following are a few examples:

Samuel Rutherford was a 17th century Scottish Presbyterian theologian and author who wrote,

> "The same power that grants authority to government also limits that authority. Rutherford in particular emphasized limited government. The people, acting under the will of God, had given the civil government only limited authority, and they had given it conditionally; they reserved the right to terminate their covenant with the ruler if the ruler violated the covenant terms. Consequently the ruler is acting without legitimate authority if he violates the laws of God and nature by suppressing the basic liberties of

the people. In such instances he is not to be obeyed. In fact, he is to be resisted. It is the Christian's duty to resist – by force if necessary." [189]

"*Lex Rex* is a book by Samuel Rutherford published in 1644 on limited government and constitutionalism. The Latin title can be translated Law [is] King and...the book's contents, opposes the doctrine of *Rex Lex* where the king himself is the law. Rutherford's refutation of *Rex Lex* was based on Deuteronomy17, and it supported the rule by law rather than rule by men... It laid the foundation for later political philosophers such as Thomas Hobbes and John Locke and thus for modern political systems such as that of the United States. After the English Restoration, the authorities burned *Lex Rex* and cited the author for high treason, which his death prevented from taking effect." [190]

Algernon Sidney was an English politician, republican political theorist, a colonel, and opponent of King Charles II of England.

"Algernon Sidney (1622-1683) served on the Council of the State of the Commonwealth under Cromwell's Protectorate in 1652. He believed... rulers exercise only such power as the people have given them, and when rulers go beyond that and usurp additional power, the people have a right to resist." [191]

---

[189] Samuel Rutherford, *Lex Rex, or the Law and the Prince*, 1644, pp.1, 6-7.

[190] *Wikipedia*, "The Law, Lex, Should Be Over the King, Rex, Deut.17, Supporting Rule of Law".

[191] John Eidsmoe, *Christianity and the Constitution*, p. 69.

Johannes Althusius, a German jurist and political philosopher in the 16th century, supported the idea that tyranny can be resisted by force, provided such resistance is used as a last resort.

> "Althusius also defends the idea that subjects should rather flee, thereby avoiding obedience by fleeing, but when manifest force is applied by the magistrate to private persons, then in case of the need to defend their lives, resistance is permitted to them." [192]

The Massachusetts Provincial Congress agreed with John Hancock, stating in late 1774:

> "Resistance to tyranny becomes the Christian and social duty of each individual.... Continue steadfast and, with a proper sense of your dependence on God, nobly defend those rights which heaven gave, and no man ought to take from us." [193]

John Milton was an English poet, scholar, and a civil servant for the Commonwealth of England under Oliver Cromwell. He wrote at a time of religious flux and political upheaval, and is best known for his epic poem Paradise Lost.

> "John Milton (1608-1674) was a political as well as a religious figure. An expert swordsman as well as a theologian, Milton defended the right to resist illegitimate usurpation of authority." [194]

---

[192] Andries Raath, "Theologico-Political Federalism: The Office of Magistracy and the Legacy of Heinrich Bullinger", *Westminster Theological Journal.* Volume 63. 2001 (2).

[193] "John Hancock, 1774". George Bancroft, *History of the United States of America,* 6 vols. (Boston: Charles C. Little and James Brown, Third Edition, 1838), Vol. II, p. 229.

[194] *Encyclopedia Britannica,* 1896, s.v. "John Milton".

Thomas Paine lived in the 18th century and received acclaim from the pamphlet he authored called "*Common Sense*". It was widely read in the Colonies at the time they declared their independence from Great Brittan.

> "He that rebels against reason is a real rebel, but he that in defense of reason rebels against tyranny has a better title to 'Defender of the Faith', than [King] George the Third." [195]

> "Many early English legal scholars such as John Locke had a profound impact on American thought. Locke claimed that the 'Word of God' as fundamental law is to be utilized as 'a rule of righteousness to influence our lives' as a concrete means of 'checking arbitrary government'." [196]

John Eidsmoe is a professor of constitutional law, an attorney, a sought-after speaker, and an author.

> "I believe fifteen basic principles which underlie the thinking of the founding fathers... which are either derived from, or at least compatible with, Christianity and the Bible. A belief that governments have only such powers as are delegated to them by the people in said covenants or compacts, and that *when governments attempt to usurp powers not so delegated, they become illegitimate and are to be resisted.* [Emphasis added]" [197]

Richard Bushman is an American historian, a professor of History emeritus at Columbia University, and an

---

[195] Thomas Paine, *The Crisis*, January 13, 1777; http://www.brainyquote.com/quotes/authors/j/john_philpot_curran.html#ixzz1mkeGlWch.

[196] J.N. Figgis, *The Divine Right of Kings*, Cambridge, 1914, p. 311.

[197] John Eidsmoe, *Christianity and the Constitution*, p.72-73.

author. He received his PhD in the History of American Civilization from Harvard University,

> "God has not subjected the lives and liberties of the ruled to the arbitrary will and pleasure of rulers. He gave laws to their authority so that they were not at liberty to pursue and accomplish their own desires. The law defined the line beyond which rulers became tyrants and resistance became a duty." [198]

> "An unjust law is no law at all, and there is a duty and obligation not to obey it."
> ~Thomas Aquinus~

Reverend John Muhlenberg was one of the Black Robed Regiment pastors who taught a powerful sermon on Ecclesiastes chapter three to his Colonial congregation. He said: "The Bible tells us there is a time for all things and there is a time to preach and a time to pray, but the time for me to preach has passed away. And there is a time to fight, and that time has come now. Now is the time to fight!"

Having said that, he took off his black robe and revealed the uniform of a Virginia Colonel. Then he took his musket from behind the pulpit, put on his hat and marched off to war with over three hundred men in his congregation who volunteered to follow him.

John Gill was a well-known English pastor, biblical scholar and theologian in the eighteenth century. He had mastered the Latin classics and learned Greek by age eleven.

---

[198] Richard L. Bushman, *From Puritan to Yankee: Character and the Social Order in Connecticut,* 1690-1765 (Cambridge: Harvard University Press) 1967, 1980, pp. 20-21.

"This is not to be understood as if the magistrates were above the laws and had a lawless power to do as they will without opposition; for they are under the law and liable to the penalty of it, in case of disobedience, as others; and when they make their own will a law, or exercise a lawless tyrannical power, in defiance of the laws of God, and of the land to the endangering of the lives, liberties, and properties of subjects, they may be resisted, as Saul was by the people of Israel, when he would have taken away the life of Jonathan for the breach of an arbitrary law of his own, and that too, without the knowledge of it; 1 Samuel 14:45... " [199]

Numerous articles are written in theological journals recognizing the right to resist oppressive government. Below is just one example.

"A totalitarian government that usurps all authority and power to itself from the family, church and other similar associations, thus overstepping God-given bounds, must be resisted. This seems to be the position of John on the island of Patmos. The Roman Emperor had transgressed his governmental limits when he demanded what is the sole prerogative of God-worship. Bennett remarks on Revelation that it is not always true that the Christian should obey the governing authorities." [200]

Power and authority are not the same. Dictators, tyrants, and despots may have power, but they have no legitimate authority because that comes only from

---

[199] John Gill, *An Exposition of the New Testament*, Vol. 6 (1852) p.116.

[200] Ronald B. Mayers, "The N.T. Doctrine of the State"; quote by Bennette Op. cit. p.31, (1969; 2002). *Journal of the Evangelical Theological Society,* Volume 12 (12:211).

God who definitely would never delegate it to those who abuse people. The following quote from *The Republic Magazine* mentions a group of people who assembled in November, 2009 to form a Continental Congress in order to address our government's abuses of the Constitution. It resulted in a plan to save our Constitution that was entitled *"Articles of Freedom"*. *(www.articlesfreedom.us)*

"Power comes from the barrel of a gun. Authority comes from being congruent [lining up] with natural or higher law [from God]. The federal government is all power and no authority. The Continental Congress of 2009 is all authority and no power. America is faced with a situation that has occurred repeatedly throughout history. The Continental Congress must now follow in the daring and noble tradition of the brave remnant who have carried the seeds of liberty through the flames of many a crumbling empire to plant them in the ash, the fertile soil of tyranny fallen. Now is the time that we must, and we will, secure a rebirth of liberty and law." [201]

"That government being instituted for the common benefit, the doctrine of nonresistance against arbitrary power and oppression is absurd, slavish, and destructive of the good and happiness of mankind." [202]

---

[201] Shaffer Cox, *Republic Magazine*, p. 16, "Alaska Delegate to the Continental Congress of 2009". [Search the web for the "Continental Congress of 2009" and *www.articlesfreedom.us*]

[202] *The Constitution of Tennessee, Article 1, Section 2*

CHAPTER 11

CONCLUSION

The Spirit of the Lord GOD is upon me... He has sent me to bind up the brokenhearted, to proclaim liberty to captives and freedom to prisoners.
Isaiah 61:1

God is the author of freedom. He gave us volition and holds us accountable for the decisions we make. We live in a world full of tyrants and despots who have enslaved most of the people on this planet. Freedom is not free, and each generation is responsible for fighting against the enemies of freedom. If we fail in this endeavor, our children and grandchildren will no longer enjoy the blessings of freedom but will suffer under the scourge of slavery.

Because it is so hard to acknowledge what our government has become, most people tend to look the other way when abuse occurs. But isn't this exactly what transpired in Germany as Hitler rose to power?

Consider this: if someone accused a member of your family of molesting a child, you would probably be offended, deny it, and maybe become angry. But what you need to do is to find out if the allegation is true. If it is, then you must get involved and take steps to make sure it never happens again. Anyone who ignores such an allegation and looks the other way to protect their guilty family member shares in their guilt and crime.

The same is true when it comes to government abuse; it is wrong to look the other way. But so many people refuse to face the reality that America is no longer the land of the free. Each one of us has the responsibility to raise our voice and sound the alarm whenever government officials try to exploit us. We must demand that our leaders obey the Constitution and we must refuse to comply with any laws that infringe on our God-given rights.

We will cease to be free if we lack the objectivity and courage to see our government as it truly is. Our society is degenerating into a cesspool of immorality. Our political leaders are systematically intruding into our privacy and violating our God-given rights. And we have been tolerating it. Why? Why are we putting up with their lies, scandals, and abuse?

Because of fear, ignorance, and apathy, because we seek security rather than freedom, because we trust government more than we trust God, because churches have become entertainment centers that focus on money and emotions more than the Word of God, because pastors have become politically correct cowards, because we have kicked God out of the school house, the court house, and the houses of Congress, and because we have been conditioned to think like slaves rather than to think and act like the independent, free men and women we can and should be.

> "How has it happened that the most courageous defenders of liberty in the world have become complacent condoners of tyranny? I place the bulk of the blame on America's pastors and preachers. For decades, they have told and retold their congregants to "trust the government', 'submit to the government', 'obey the government', 'the government is good', 'the government is of God', etc. They have bastardized

Romans 13 and helped turn free men and women into sheepish slaves of the state." [203]

We, as a nation, have rejected the Lord and have no fear or concern that He will also reject us. We no longer trust in Him. We have not resisted evil in our society or in our government. We have surrendered our morality, our conscience, and our freedoms without even putting up a fight. Consequently, we now have the kind of society and government we deserve.

We are foolish to expect life to get better until we muster the courage and will to stand for righteousness and to resist evil. Until we do, the Lord will not be on our side. We will continue our downward spiral into ruin and things will get worse, much worse. Judge Andrew Napolitano summarized our situation very well:

> "It is dangerous to be right when the government is wrong because government in America today is not logic or reason, it is not fidelity to the Constitution, and it is not compliance with the Rule of Law. Rather, it is force. Government today steals liberty and property in the name of safety. It restricts your ability to express yourself, to defend yourself, to be yourself; and it uses fear to keep the people submissive.
>
> "Government rejects its moral and legal obligations, insulates itself from litigation, breaks its own laws, makes its own rules, declares worthless paper to be money, and then devalues even that. Government will not hesitate to use force upon those who challenge it. Government has made it unlawful to resist its use

---

[203] Chuck Baldwin, "Americans Putting the Noose Around Their Own Necks", By October 4, 2012, Archived column:
http://chuckbaldwinlive.com/home/archives/5164

of force even when those uses are patently and unconditionally wrong." [204]

What a mess! But it's not too late. We can still be delivered if our hope is in the Lord. Our problems are not too big for Him. He can break the shackles of bondage that have been forged against us.

> "America has strayed from its godly roots and replaced God's absolute moral standards with those that seem right to a man but are wholly destructive of our moral fabric. We must turn back to God, reject this man-made ethic grounded in covetousness, envy and greed, and recommit ourselves to godly values and right living." [205]

Even though we have been fed a steady diet of lies and propaganda that offer false solutions, we still have the ability to think for ourselves and seek truth. You have been asked 215 questions to motivate you to come to your own conclusions concerning your relationship with your government and your God.

Tolerating Tyranny is not a manual that gives specific details on how to take our country back and reclaim our freedom. It doesn't tell you what to do because that is your decision and between you and the Lord. You have the freedom to do whatever you think is right. We all are responsible to stand for righteousness and resist evil. We have God's Word, the Holy Spirit, our conscience, the Constitution, and the words of the brave souls who have gone before us to encourage us and guide us.

---

[204] Judge Andrew P. Napolitano, *It Is Dangerous To Be Right When the Government Is Wrong*, p. 63.

[205] David Limbaugh, "Dr. Carson's Good Medicine", *Human Events*, 2-12-13.

You have been challenged to consider quotes from the Bible and from brave independent patriots who faced the **same issues we are facing. Don't let** fear **defeat you; don't let it neutralize your motivation to stand for freedom** or to stop you from doing what you know is right.

> *The LORD is my light and my salvation; whom shall I fear? The LORD is the strength of my life; of whom shall I be afraid?* **Psalm 27:1**

> *Fear thou not; for I am with thee: be not dismayed; for I am thy God: I will strengthen thee; yea, I will help thee; yea, I will uphold thee with the right hand of my righteousness.* (KJV) **Isaiah 41:10**

> *The LORD is on my side; I will not fear. What can man do to me?* **Psalm 118:6**

We must stop putting our trust in political parties and politicians who have deceived us. We must refuse to be duped any longer by the media. We must learn to think like free men and women. And most importantly, we must trust in the Lord, our God, for deliverance.

> *It is better to trust in the Lord than to put confidence in man. 9) It is better to take refuge in the Lord than to trust in princes.* **Psalm 118:8-9**

> *Do not trust in princes, in mortal man, in whom there is no salvation.* **Psalm 146:3**

> *Cursed is the man who trusts in mankind and makes flesh his strength, and whose heart turns away from the Lord.* **Jeremiah 17:5**

Even the best of men will let you down sooner or later, but the Lord never will. We have His word on it.

For He Himself has said, "I will never leave you nor forsake you." 6) So we may boldly say: "The Lord is my helper; I will not fear. What can man do to me? <u>Hebrews 13:5a-6</u>

God is our refuge and strength, a very present help in trouble. <u>Psalm 46:1</u>

O Lord, my strength and my stronghold, and my refuge in the day of distress. <u>Jeremiah 16:19</u>

The Lord is my rock and my fortress and my deliverer, My God, my rock, in whom I take refuge; my shield and the horn of my salvation, my stronghold. <u>Psalm 18:2</u>

Behold, the eye of the Lord is on those who fear [respect] Him, on those who hope for His loving kindness, 19) to deliver their soul from death and to keep them alive in famine. 20) Our soul waits for the Lord; He is our help and our shield. <u>Psalm 33:18-20</u>

HERE'S WHAT GOD TOLD ANCIENT ISRAEL TO DO TO SAVE THEIR NATION:

If my people who are called by my name humble themselves, and pray and seek my face and turn from their wicked ways, then I will hear from heaven and will forgive their sin and heal their land. <u>2 Chronicles 7:14</u>

We have instructions from the God of the Universe on how a dying nation can be healed. If He could save Israel, He can save America. If we will humble ourselves, pray, seek Him and turn from our wicked ways, He will bless this nation once again with freedom and prosperity.

EPILOGUE

Only God can provide real and lasting solutions to our problems and only He can save us to the utmost, not only from abusive power, but from the greatest problem of all, our sin problem. He has already provided that solution.

He sent His Son, Jesus Christ, to the cross in our place to take the punishment that we deserve. He died there, was buried, and then rose from the grave in order to offer eternal life to anyone who puts his total trust in Him. Salvation is a GIFT that is given to anyone who will trust in Christ and His atoning work on the cross rather than trusting in his own puny works to be saved.

> *For by grace you have been saved through faith, and that not of yourselves; it is the GIFT of God, 9) not of* **works, lest anyone should boast."** Ephesians 2:8-9

> *For the wages of sin is death, but the FREE GIFT of God is eternal life through Christ Jesus our Lord.* Romans 6:23

No one can work for a gift because a gift is free. The way one receives the gift of salvation is by simply believing in Jesus Christ.

When a Philippian jailer asked the Apostle Paul, "What must I do to be saved?" Paul told him to "believe in the Lord Jesus Christ and you will be saved…." Acts 16:31 If you have not believed in Him as your Savior, you can do it right now and receive eternal life. Do it right **now before it's too late!**

*"**He who believes in the Son** <u>has</u> everlasting life; and he who does not believe the Son shall not see **life, but the wrath of God abides on him.**"* <u>John 3:36</u>

If you want to hear more, go to the Country Bible **Church's website** and click on the big red button on the homepage. All audios, visuals, live streaming, and publications on the website are free.

<u>www.countrybiblechurch.us</u>

BIBLIOGRAPHY

Adams, John Quincy. Reprinted in J. Wingate Thornton, *Vol. I Christian History of the Constitution* (1860).

Anderson, Tom. *Sil**ence Is Not Golden**, **It's Yellow**,* Western Islands.

Baldwin Chuck and Timothy. *Romans 13, The True Meaning of Submission.*

Baldwin, Chuck. **"The Fear of God Is Not in This Place",** Archived Column, July 19, 2012.

Bardolph, Richard. **"Some Reflections on Civil Disobedience,"** *Concordia Theological Monthly* 38, no. 6 (June 1967). Barton, David. *Celebrate Liberty! Famous Patriotic Speeches & Sermons,* (WallBuilders Press, Aledo, Texas, 2003).

Bastiat, Frederic. "The Law, 1998, The Foundation for Economic Education", *Christianity and Civilization,* Geneva Divinity School Press, 1983.

Black's Law Dictionary, Abridged Fifth Edition, West Publishing Co., 1983.

Blackstone, Sir William. *Commentaries on the Laws of New England,* 5 volumes, 1771, 1:38 39, 42.

Bodin. *On Sovereignty: Six Books on the Commonwealth.*

Boryszewski, Ralph. *The Constitution That Never Was,* 1995, xviii.

"Boston Tea Party, 1774, Report of the Crown appointed Governor of Boston, Massachusetts, sent to the Board of Trade in England". Hezekiah Niles, *Principles and Acts of the Revolution in America* (Baltimore: William Ogden Niles, 1822).

Bushman, Richard L. *From Puritan to Yankee: Character and the Social Order to Connecticut,* 1690 1765.

Calvin, John. *Commentaries on the Epistle of Paul the Apostle to the Romans,* (1539), John Owen translation (1849).

Carson, D. A. *New Bible Commentary: 21st Century Edition,* Rev. Ed. of: *The New Bible Commentary, 3rd Ed.* /Edited by D. Guthrie, J.A. Motyer. 1970, 4th ed. (Leicester, England; Downers Grove, Ill., USA: Inter Varsity Press, 1994), Ro 12:9.

Chambers, Whittaker. *Witness* (New York Random House), 1952.

Cicero, Marcus Tullius. *Orations of Marcus Tullius Cicero,* Colonial Press, (1900).

Citizens Rule Book, Jury Handbook.

Cox, Shaeffer. "Alaskan Delegate to the Continental Congress of 2009", *Republic Magazine.* [Search the web for the **"Continental Congress of 2009" and** *www.articlesfreedom.us*]

Cushing, H. *The Writings of Samuel Adams,* v.3, N.Y. ed., 1904.

"Declaration of Right**s**", October 14, 1774, *Journals of the Continental Congress*, 1774 1789.

The Economic Collapse Blog, March 7, 2013.

Eidsmoe, John. *Christianity and the Constitution—The Faith of Our Founding Fathers* (Grand Rapids, MI: Baker).

Fox Business News, John Stossell Show, The Students for Liberty Conference, February 22, 2013.

Eidsmoe, John. *God and Caesar, Biblical Faith and Political Action,* Wipf and Stock Publishers.

Eichmann, John K. *Grace Military Ministries Bible Study Newsletter.*

Encyclopedia Britannica, **1896, s.v.** "John Milton".

Farmer, Brian. "Is Soaking the Rich the Right Answer", *The New American,* March 4, 2013.

Federer, W. J. (2001). *Great Quotations: A Collection of Passages, Phrases, and Quotations Influencing Early and Modern World History,* Referenced according to their Sources in Literature, Memoirs, Letters, Governmental Documents, Speeches, Charters, Court Decisions and Constitutions; St. Louis, MO: *AmeriSearch.*

Figgis J.N., *The Divine Right of Kings,* Cambridge, 1914.

Fish, H. C., *Encyclopedia of 7700 Illustrations: Signs of the Times, Paul Lee Tan,* (Garland, TX: Bible Communications, Inc., 1996).

Frame, John M. "The Institutes of Biblical Law", Review Article in *Westminster Theological Journal,* Volume 38, 1975 (2) (196).

Gardoski, K. "Jesus and War". in Vol. 14: *Journal of Ministry and Theology* (2010). (1) (16–17). Clarks Summit, PA: Baptist Bible College.

Geisler, Norman L.A. "Premillennial View of Law and Government", *Bibliotheca Sacra,* Volume142, 567 (Dallas, TX: Dallas Theological Seminary, 1985), 262.

Grant, Michael. *The Twelve Caesars,* (1975).

Gray, William. "Is There Anything That Can Be Done To Save The United States", *Worldview Weekend,* 8-29-12.

Gill, John. *An Exposition of the New Testament,* Vol. 6 (1852).

Haldane, Robert. *"Fear of Controversy",* 1874.

Hamilton, Alexander. *Federalist Papers # 65* (1787).

Hancock, John. 1774. George Bancroft, *History of the United States of America,* 6 vols. (Boston: Charles C. Little and James Brown, Third Edition, 1838), Vol. II.

Hancock, John. In an **"Oration on the Boston Massacre,** March 5. **1774"**, *The Magazine of History, with Notes and Queries,* Vol. 24, No. 95 (1923), pp 125, 136.

Hand, Learned. (1872-1961), "Judge, U. S. court of Appeals". http://quotes.libertytree.ca/quote_blog/Learned.Hand.Quote.B58E

Harrison, E.F. **"Romans"**, in **The Expositor's Bible Commentary**, vol. 10, ed. F.E. Gabelein (Grand Rapids: Zondervan, 1976).

Henry, M. Matthew. **Henry's** *Commentary on the Whole Bible: Complete and Unabridged in One Volume* (Rom 13:1-6), (1994), Peabody: Hendrickson.

Hodge, Charles. *Commentary on the Epistle to the Romans,* 1886 reprint, Grand Rapids: Wm. B. Eerdmans Publishing Co., 1947.

Hoops, Rev. Christopher. *The Battle of Lexington,* Roseville, California Theology Editor, Nordskog Publishing.

House, H. Wayne. *Christian Ministries and The Law:* Revised edition (26), Grand Rapids, Mich.: (1999). Kregel.

House, H. Wayne. *The Duty of Civil Disobedience to the Government: Contemporary Struggles Between Christians and the State.*

Humphrey Deward F. *Nationalism and Religion in America,* 1774-1789, (1924).

Jay, John. 1st Chief Justice U.S. Supreme Court, 1789; quote is recorded in an early Supreme Court Decision which Jay would have written. The decision is *Georgia vs. Brailsford 3 US* (3 Dall.) 1, 4 (1794).

Johnson, Alan. "The Bible and War in America: An Historical Survey", *Journal of the Evangelical Theological Society.* Vol. 28: 1985 (2) (178–179). Lynchburg, VA: The Evangelical Theological Society.

Kopel, David B. *The Torah and Self-Defense.*

Kopel, David B. *The Human Right of Self-Defense.*

Levin, Mark. *The Liberty Amendments,* Threshold Editions, 2013.

Locke, John. *Of Civil Government,* (1689).

Longley, Robert. "About Guide to U.S. Government", *About.com.us government info*

Limbaugh, David. **Dr. Carson's Good Medicine, Human Events:** 2-12-13.

Luther, Martin. "To the Emperor at the Diet of Worms, 'Here I Stand Speech'", (1521), *Conservative Theological Journal* Volume 2. 1998 (4) (54), Fort Worth, TX: Tyndale Theological Seminary.

Luther, Martin. **Luther's** *Cat. Writings.*

Maharrey, Mike. "Rasmussen Poll: Nullification Goes Mainstream", *Tenth Amendment Center,* May 6 2013

Marshall, Peter and David Manuel, *The Glory of America* (Bloomington, MN: **Garborg's Heart 'N Home, Inc.,**'91), 2.5.

Matheson, William. "Justice in the Social Order", *Westminster Theological Journal,* Volume 08. 1945 (2) (145–146). Philadelphia: Westminster Theological Seminary.

Maybury, Richard J. *Ancient Rome, How It Affects You Today,* 2004, Bluestocking, Press.

Mayers, Ronald B. "The N.T. Doctrine of the State", Quote by Bennette Op. cit. p.31, The Evangelical Theological Society. (1969; 2002). *Journal of the Evangelical Theological Society,* Volume 12 (12:211).

Mayhew, Jon**athan. 1749,** "**T**o the Council and House of Representatives in Colonial New England". Dorothy Dimmick, "Why Study the Election Sermons of Our **Founding Generation?**" San Francisco, CA: *The American Christian Prompter,* Winter 1993, Vol. 4, No. 2.

Mayhew, Jonathan. January 30, 1750, in the sermon, "**A** Discourse Concerning Unlimited Submission and Non-resistance to the **Higher Powers, etc., etc.**" *The Annals of America,* 20 vols. (Chicago, IL: *Encyclopedia Britannica,* 1968), Vol. 1.

Mazzini, Giuseppe. *The Duties of Man,* (1805-1872).

Merryman, Ron. *The Protection of Conscience: The Bible and Government* (2009).

Minister Mayhew, Jonathan, of Boston. *Sermon,* 1766.

Napolitano, Judge Andrew P. *It Is Dangerous To Be Right When the Government Is Wrong.*

Niles, Hezekiah. "**Boston Tea Party** 1774, Report of the Crown-appointed Governor of Boston, Massachusetts, Sent to the Board **of Trade in England**". *Principles and Acts of the Revolution in America* (Baltimore: William Ogden Niles, 1822).

Otis, James. *The Rights of British Colonies Asserted and Proved* (1764).

Paine, Thomas. *The Crisis,* Dec. 23, 1776.

Paul, Ron. *The Office of Representative Ron Paul,* January 30, 1997.

Plaster, David L. "The Christian and War: A Matter of Personal Conscience", Vol. 6: *Grace Theological Journal.* 1985 (447). Winona, IN: Grace Seminary.

Pope, Randy. *http://lwhf.com/black_regiment.html*

Powers, Peter. Election Sermon entitled "Jesus Christ the King", (Newburyport, 1778). Shipton, Clifford K., **Sibley's Harvard Graduates** (Boston: Massachusetts Historical Society, 1965), Vol. XIII.

Raath, Andries. "Theologico-Political Federalism: The Office of Magistracy and the Legacy of Heinrich Bullinger", *Westminster Theological Journal*, Volume 63. 2001 (2) (302). Philadelphia: Westminster Theological Seminary.

Rawls, John. *A Theory of Justice,* (Cambridge, Mass.; Harvard University Press, 1971).

Rolling Stone Magazine, **"The GOP War on Voting"**, retrieved 4-7-2012, *http://en.wikipedia.org/wiki/Voting_fraud,*

Rose, Tom. *The Journal of Christian Reconstruction,* Vol. 5, No. 1 (Summer © 1978).

Rose, Tom. "Our Reconstruction and the American Republic", *Christianity and Civilization,* Geneva Divinity School Press, 1983.

Rousas, John Rushdoony. *This Independent Republic,* Ross House Books, 1964.

Rutherford, Samuel. *Lex Rex, or the Law and the Prince,* 1644.

Selden, John. *Dictionary of Burning Words of Brilliant Writers: A Cyclopedia from the Literature of All Ages* (1895).

Stream, Carol. *Reformation and Revival,* Vol. 3: 1994 (1) (116Illinois: Reformation and Revival Ministries*)*.
Telushkin, Rabbi Joseph. *Biblical Literacy: The Most Important People, Events, and Ideas of the Hebrew Bible* (1997), p. xxi.

"The Commission on Theology and Church Relations of the Lutheran Church", *Missouri Synod*, **379. ("Civil Obedience & Disobedience").**

Thieme Jr., R.B. *Laws of Divine Establishment.*

Thompson, Arthur R. "The Problem with Local Regionalization", *The JBS Bulletin*, June 2012.

Thompson, Arthur R. "War, War, War", *JBS Bulletin,* March 2012.

Tucker, George. *On The Study of Law,* (**Editor's Note: Blackstone's Commentaries: With Notes of Reference, to** the Constitution and Laws, of the Federal Government of the United States; and the Commonwealth of Virginia 5 Vols. 1803 – reprinted in View of the Constitution of the United States with Selective Writings 1999).

Tucker, John. Minister of Newbury, Mass. *Election Sermon, 1771.*

Wallace, George B. **"Proper Use of the U.S. Military"**, *The New American Magazine*, July 5, 2010.

Walvoord, J. F., Zuck, R. B., *The Bible Knowledge Commentary: An Exposition of the Scriptures* (1 Pet. 2:13–15). Dallas Theological Seminary. (1985). Wheaton, IL: Victor Books.

Weisman, Charles A. *Life, Liberty, and Property,* by Weisman Publications 1997.

Whitehead, John H. *Christian Resistance In the Face of State Interference, Christianity and Civilization,* Geneva Divinity School.

Witherspoon, John. Edward Frank Humphrey. *Nationalism and Religion* (Boston: Chipman Law Publishing Co., 1924).

Witherspoon, John. May 17, 1776, in his sermon entitled, **"The Dominion of Providence over the Passions of Men."** Varnum Lansing Collins, President Witherspoon (*New York: Arno Press and The New York Times,* 1969), I:197-8.

Williams, Gregory, **"Romans 13 & Christ's Clergy Response Teams"**, *NewsWithViews.com,* 1-21-09.

Wilson, James M. *The Establishment and Limits of Civil Government,* (1883).

Wines, E.C., *Commentaries on the Laws of the Ancient Hebrews* with an "Introductory Essay on Civil Society and Government", (1853).

Witmer, John A. *Bibliotheca Sacra Volume 133* (133:532); Dallas Theological Seminary (1976; 2002), *Bibliotheca Sacra* Volume 142, 1985. Dallas, TX: Dallas Theological Seminary.

Woods, Andy. *Darwin, Evolution, and the American Constitution,* March 2011.

Wood, Gordon. *Creation of the American Republic* (1969).

Wood Jr., James E. "The American Tradition in Church and State", Vol. 5: *Ashland Theological Journal,* 1972 (10). Ashland, OH: Ashland Theological Seminary.